D1399479

"While many churches are looking to survive the complexities of the first part of the twenty-first century, McIntosh and Reeves address key systems to help churches not only survive, but thrive. Church leaders: applying the methods in *Thriving Churches in the Twenty-First Century* may just stimulate you and your church to new heights."

—WILL H. MCRANEY, JR.
Associate Professor of Evangelism
New Orleans Baptist Theological Seminary

"*Thriving Churches* is excellent. Having pastored a megachurch for over twenty years, I've come to believe that certain values and practices are absolutely necessary for effective ministry. Gary, a seasoned pastor and church planter, and Dan, a skilled consultant, have clearly identified ten life-giving systems. I plan to use this book with our church staff to reassess our ministry and mission."

—DR. GARY D. KINNAMAN
Senior Pastor
Word of Grace Church, Mesa, Arizona

"The uniqueness of this contribution is that the authors are both veteran consultants who combine keen observation and discerning analysis. They apply systems-theory thinking to the life of the local church in a comprehensive manner. I warmly commend their work as providing in-depth analysis together with a wealth of practical guidance."

—EDDIE GIBBS
Donald A. McGavran Professor of Church Growth
Fuller Theological Seminary

"Gary McIntosh and Dan Reeves must be two of the ten people in our land who know the most about churches and the proven ways for churches to navigate their future. In this readable and practical volume, the two authors reflect on the future that appears to be emerging, and they explain ten of the 'hinges' that will swing tens of thousands of churches into the kind of future that God wants for them."

—GEORGE G. HUNTER
Distinguished Professor of Evangelization
Asbury Theological Seminary

thriving churches
in the twenty-first century

God bless your life and ministry -

Gary L. McIntosh

10-1-06

thriving churches
in the twenty-first century

10 LIFE-GIVING SYSTEMS
FOR VIBRANT MINISTRY

Gary L. McIntosh &
R. Daniel Reeves

Kregel
Academic & Professional

Thriving Churches in the Twenty-First Century: 10 Life-Giving Systems for Vibrant Ministry

© 2006 by Gary L. McIntosh and R. Daniel Reeves

Published by Kregel Publications, a division of Kregel, Inc., P.O. Box 2607, Grand Rapids, MI 49501.

Library of Congress Cataloging-in-Publication Data
McIntosh, Gary.
   Thriving churches in the twenty-first century: 10 life-giving systems for vibrant ministry / by Gary L. McIntosh and R. Daniel Reeves.
     p.   cm.
   Includes bibliographical references and index.
   1. Church renewal. 2. Pastoral theology. I. Reeves, R. Daniel. II. Title.
BV600.3.M354   2006   253—dc22   2005035944

ISBN 0-8254-3170-0

Printed in the United States of America

06 07 08 09 10 / 5 4 3 2 1

Contents

Revitalization and Change at Four Critical Points

Critical Point A: Generating Spiritual Energy

Critical Point B: Developing Effective Leaders

Critical Point C: Increasing People Flow

Critical Point D: Charting Amid Change

Acknowledgments

My thanks go to our editors at Kregel, Jim Weaver and Moriah Sharp. Their hard work helped create a more polished book, and I greatly appreciate them both. It has also been my delight to work together with my great friend, Dan Reeves. His views on ministry and life have always been insightful, and I treasure our friendship.

—GARY L. MCINTOSH

The person who is most dear to me and who has contributed immeasurably to the insights in these pages is my wife and ultimate companion, Ethelwynne. As a tenured communications professor and daughter of English pastor/evangelist Joe Blinco, Ethelwynne is a multitalented, full partner who is vicariously trained in all that I believe and offer. Among those who invested in me early, none can match my parents, Max and Marjorie Reeves, and my youth pastor, Robert Deal. Most recently, those who have encouraged Ethelwynne and me the most are our friends, comrades, and neighbors, David and Tonya Miller, and the pastors of the Lake Erie Classis of the Reformed Church in America.

I have also been blessed beyond measure by outstanding mentors, beginning with a dramatic call into ministry at the age of twenty-two. Fifteen men invested personal time with me at critical points: Bill Bright, Joe Blinco, Bud Hinkson, John Wimber, Donald McGavran, Charles Kraft, Peter Wagner, Ralph Winter, Edwin Orr, Doug Hartman, Robert Clinton, Tom Paterson, Wayne Cordeiro, Erwin McManus, and Charles Van Engen.

Finally, I have been privileged to work alongside some of the brightest and most devoted leaders in the church world as associates or partners in various projects. A small portion of the wisdom contained in both their books and their lives has been transferred to me by osmosis. The most significant twenty are Dave Travis, Bill Easum, Carl George, Howard Snyder, George Hunter, Gary McIntosh, Eddie Gibbs, Elmer Towns, Michael Horton, David Neff, Kevin Mannoia, Bill Donahue, Paul Chappell, James Furr, Timothy George, Doug Slaybaugh, Doug Pagitt, Daniel Allen, Todd Hunter, and Roberta Hestenes.

—R. Daniel Reeves

There's a Whole Lot of Shaking Going On

On the morning of June 28, 1992, I awoke with a jolt. All of us who were within two hundred miles of Landers, California, were awakened by the largest earthquake occurring in Southern California in more than twenty-five years. My wife and I (Dan) felt only a mild rattle at our home in Santa Maria, but our daughter, Rachel, was on summer staff at Forest Home Christian Conference Center. That was a mere fourteen miles from Landers—the epicenter—so the quake got our immediate attention.

Turning on the TV to get further reports didn't relieve my concern. We heard that another large quake had hit Big Bear Lake, California, and Forest Home is situated exactly midpoint between the epicenters of the two quakes.

Although Forest Home and my daughter were a bit shaken, they were blessed to have survived the two quakes. In the canyon at Landers, though, physical changes occurred that will last for many generations. I visited the area a few weeks later. A friend showed me a boulder the size of a UPS delivery van that had fallen from the peak of the canyon into someone's back yard. The boulder had bounced fifty feet off the ground, snipping off the tops of huge pine trees as though they were toothpicks. Now that's awesome power! It was a classic case of "good news–bad news" for the poor fellow who went out at sunrise to inspect the damage to his property. The good news was that the boulder stopped ten feet short of his house. The bad news was that his landscape will likely contain this oversized, and certainly unwelcome, rock forever! It's just too big to move.

During the past few years, a similar power has been vibrating the North American church in ways that have also changed its landscape forever. The writings of Peter Drucker, Lyle Schaller, Leith Anderson, Faith Popcorn, Leonard Sweet, Peter Senge, Joel Barker, Stanley Davis, Greg Ogden, Alvin Toeffler, Bill Easum, Tom Bandy, Erwin McManus, and others tell us that today's churches are in a seismically active period. In case you missed them, the following are a few comments from these insightful leaders.

Peter Drucker, one of the leading experts on management, states,

> Every few hundred years in Western history there occurs a sharp transformation. We cross a "divide." Within a few short decades, society rearranges itself—its worldview; its basic values; its social and political structure; its arts; its key institutions. Fifty years later, there is a new world. And the people born then cannot even imagine the world in which their grandparents lived and into which their own parents were born. We are currently living through just such a transformation.[1]

One of the most creative voices in American business circles, Tom Peters, declares,

> Revolution? The word is not too strong. And it's not the same thing as change. Change? Change? Yes, we've almost all, finally, embraced the notion that "change is the only constant." Well, sorry. Forget change! The word is feeble. Keep saying "revolution." If it doesn't roll easily off your tongue, then I suggest you have a perception

problem—and, more to the point, a business or a career problem. What we do. What we make. How we work. Each is the subject of nothing less than a revolution.[2]

Joel Barker, a key spokesperson for changing paradigms in business, notes,

> We have been living in a time when fundamental rules, the basic ways we do things, have been altered dramatically. That is, what was right and appropriate in the early '60s is now, in many cases, wrong and highly inappropriate. Or, conversely, what was impossible, crazy, or clearly out of line in the early '60s, is, in many cases today, so ordinary that we forget that it wasn't always that way. These kinds of dramatic changes are extremely important because they have created in us a special sense of impermanence that generates tremendous discomfort.[3]

These leaders are obviously talking about life in general and business in particular. But parallel dynamics are also taking place in Christianity. Lyle Schaller, America's foremost church consultant, suggests,

> What is the number one issue facing Christian organizations on the North American continent today? The need to initiate and implement planned change from within an organization. The big issue is change. The central issue in any effective strategy for numerical growth is change. Reversing a period of numerical decline requires changes. Numerical growth also produces change.[4]

One of the leading pastors in the United States, Leith Anderson, writes,

> We are experiencing enormous structural change in our country and in our work—change that promises to be

greater than the invention of the printing press, greater than the Industrial Revolution, and greater than the rise and demise of communism. Our world is changing so quickly that we can barely keep track of what is happening, much less figure out how to respond.[5]

The growing consensus of these leaders is that the vibrations in the church landscape are not the result of normal generational changes, such as transfer of leadership from one generation to the next. Rather, these vibrations herald cataclysmic changes in the church. We as church leaders and Christians ignore these changes to our own peril.

All Things Have Become Topsy-Turvy

California averages about twenty earthquakes a day, including one serious, damaging earthquake every four-and-a-half years that can rearrange the landscape in seconds. The 1994 Northridge quake, which lasted twenty seconds, caused about $12.5 billion in residential damage, and many neighborhoods no longer look like they did in 1993. Much like the results of the regular, small tremors along the California landscape, changes to the church terrain, too, normally occur gradually. But occasionally even the church encounters times of explosive changes.

Before the 1950s, changes in the church progressed so slowly that church leaders had ample time to react. Following the conversion of Emperor Constantine in A.D. 312, for example, the church experienced twelve hundred years of gradual change until the events of the Reformation in the sixteenth century. Following the Reformation, the church fell back into another period of slow change that lasted for two hundred years until the First (ca. 1735–1743) and Second (ca. 1795–1830) Great Awakenings. The periods of gradual change between cataclysmic changes have, however, become increasingly shorter. Since World War II, churches have experienced almost continual turbulence occurring in the seismic range, consisting of revolution, reformation, or a megaparadigm shift. The cumulative effect of these changes on the church may eventually rival the impact of Martin Luther's momentous posting of the Ninety-five Theses in Wittenberg. Today, the changes flash so quickly about the church world that it has almost no time to react. Consider, for example, how much our perceptions are being shaken constantly by the technological advances that enable us to be confronted simultaneously with breaking news of terrorism, tidal waves, hurricanes, genocides, famines, and nuclear proliferation. How can our minds process all of these complex disturbances, let alone respond instinctively with appropriate interventions?

Today, the changes flash so quickly about the church world that it has almost no time to react.

When things begin to shake in earthquake country, those of us who live there, if we are wise, review our plans to survive "the big one." We check our stock of flashlights, battery-operated radios, and bottled water and test the safety straps on our water heaters. To ignore the messages of smaller quakes is to court future disaster.

It is likewise important that the church react as times change. It must constantly monitor its mission to bring the message of Jesus Christ to new generations and new cultures. Although the transforming power of the biblical message and the urgency of Christ's mandate to make disciples does not change, the situations in which they are proclaimed and the ways they are articulated, communicated, taught, and acted upon may change and vary. This thought is not new. Paul declared that he wanted to be all things to all people so that he could reach some (1 Cor. 9:19–23). Others throughout Christian history met changing times with innovation, imagination, and intentional action to help propagate and establish Christ's church. In the First Great Awakening, for example, John Wesley engaged his changing times by building ministry around an itinerant system of traveling lay preachers, and the innovative use of a society-class-band system of discipleship.[6]

Although the transforming power of the biblical message and the urgency of Christ's mandate to make disciples does not change, the situations in which they are proclaimed and the ways they are articulated, communicated, taught, and acted upon may change and vary.

It's unfortunate, though, that the average church ignores the shaking and the signs, and operates as though nothing will change. Unless the church has a survival plan and starts to retrofit for its own "big one," many congregations will not survive.

Restoring the Power

A few years ago, several states in the western United States experienced what is called the "blackout of 1996." The blackout doubleheader first struck in July, when two million customers were left without electricity. A month later, on Saturday, August 10, 1996, a high-tension wire expanded in southern Oregon and touched a tree, creating an enormous shutdown of electricity in several western states.

In a moment, the fragility of interlocking technology was exposed. Emergency systems failed, and the power outage resulted in a domino effect, eventually leaving 7.5 million customers in the dark. Twelve southern California hospitals shut down services. The Los Angeles County emergency headquarters were unable to contact paramedics. Six million gallons of sewage was spewed into Santa Monica Bay. People found themselves unable to do routine chores such as filling a prescription, buying gasoline, purchasing groceries, or even in some places washing their hands, because the faucets were hooked to electronic eyes. "Our society is evolving to a complex system of systems," noted Bryan Gabbard, associate director of the science and technology division for Rand Corporation, a Santa Monica–based think tank. "This interlinking controls the day-to-day activities of our work life. I don't know what caused the power failure, but it had a massive impact because of this interlinking."[7] When one area is affected, everything is affected.

The power failure might have, however, actually been a blessing in this case. Darlene Isbell, assistant director of Los Angeles County's emergency communications systems suggested, "This allows us to isolate a problem and ask, What does a loss of power do to us? That's something that is often hard to do when there is an earthquake and a number of systems, like water, power, staffing, and structural problems, happen all at once."[8]

Seven years later, on August 14, 2003, a blackout occurred in the northeastern United States. With electrons traveling through the system at 186,000 miles per second, it took less than three minutes for the outage to spread across 9,300 square miles of North America, from Detroit to Cleveland to New York. Commenting on the complexity of the interlinked system, Kristen Baird of Ohio-based First Energy Corporation noted, "You have a variety of companies with a variety of different types of facilities and you have to collect the data from each of them and then compare. You have to see what circuit went down when, what other systems were doing right before and after it went down, and compare. It's extremely, extremely complex."[9]

These regional ripples now seem small when compared with the national and global reactions that were ignited by the terrorist attacks on the Twin Towers in September 2001. Or, the subsequent attacks within several years in Madrid and London. Who could have anticipated that during this same time period there would also be unprecedented systemic ripples from a powerful tsunami in Indonesia and two devastating hurricanes in the Gulf of Mexico? The double poundings from Katrina and Rita in 2005 caused total system failures in New Orleans, plus unprecendented chaos and damage through the huge territory from eastern Texas to southern Alabama.[10] Government agencies and the general public were also shaken to the core with feelings of disgust, weariness, embarrassment, outrage, and vulnerability.

As the acceleration of extreme blackouts, terrorist attacks, and natural disasters of this past decade has demonstrated, continued functioning is not dependent upon any one system but is the result of them all "interlinking." So it is in the church. The secret to a vital, functioning ministry is the interlinking or interrelating of life-giving systems.

In a healthy human body, too, all of the systems need to be functioning. The neurological, cardiovascular, muscular, digestive, reproductive, and immune systems interact. It is not sufficient to have a healthy set of lungs if the arterial system is broken down; all of the life-giving systems need to interlink and interact to produce life. Similarly, our (Dan and Gary) experience in both individual churches and group consultations point out the need to understand the church as a "system of life-giving systems." Our observations underscore that a church's life-giving systems becoming healthy and effective has a ripple effect on the rest of the system. The synergism creates unstoppable spiritual energy. God's Spirit is at work. The Power is restored!

> . . . a church's life-giving systems becoming healthy and effective has a ripple effect on the rest of the system. The synergism creates unstoppable spiritual energy. God's Spirit is at work. The Power is restored!

Ten Life-Giving Systems

As churches position themselves for healthy, growing ministry in the new millennium, pastors, church leaders, and key laypersons must understand the conditions that are creating the changes that will affect the church. But more importantly, these people need to be intentional in how they respond.

In this book, we introduce ten life-giving systems that, if working synergistically, will help bring revitalized and robust ministry to a church that is seeking to respond to change. Many other books contain strategies for promoting growth or health in particular aspects of a church. But as with quakes, blackouts, terrorism, natural disasters, and the human body, what affects one area of the church body will affect all areas.

The critical life-giving systems discussed in this book—and their necessary interaction—have not been developed hastily. On the contrary, these systems have become clear to us in more than twenty years of consulting and working with churches in solving problems and developing visions and strategic plans for reaching their missions.

I (Gary) have had the opportunity to interact with hundreds of seminary students and midcareer pastors as professor of Christian Ministry and Leadership at Talbot School of Theology, Biola University, in La Mirada, California. I have met countless others in workshops and in consultations with churches in fifty-five different denominations. I've also reflected on a variety of church issues—generational change, evangelism and assimilation, and the effect of church size on ministry—in my books and articles.

As a missiologist, I (Dan) have seen the church at work in not only the United States but also Europe, where more than twenty-five years ago I started my ministry on a team.[11] Coming full circle from those days in Europe, I now help American churches address some of the same post-Christian attitudes that existed among university students then.[12] In my role for more than a decade as consultant with the Fuller Institute in Pasadena, and more recently as founder of the Institute for Missional Leadership Teams (IMLT) and Reeves Strategic Consultation Services, I've had the privilege of consulting with, mentoring, and coaching hundreds of pastors, leadership teams, congregations, and denominations.[13]

One of the services that I've developed is Congregational Cluster Consultations. In 1987, Lee Eliason—a close friend and pastor of a large Southern California church, now provost of Bethel Seminary—challenged me to find a way for smaller churches to benefit from the consultation process in the way that his church had. Because of this challenge, the Cluster Consultation—a high-touch, hands-on consultation experience for pastors in small and midsized churches—was born. Since the late 1980s, I've had the privilege of bringing together clusters of seven to twelve pastors of smaller churches, who had made a commitment to come together for two years to work on a plan for revitalizing their churches. Each cluster agreed to meet monthly for a full day of training and to complete assignments prior to the meeting. Initially, fifty-five churches agreed to participate in pilot clusters for a period of two years. Four of these were denominational clusters grouping pastors from specific denominational districts. Since then, more than three hundred churches have participated in these clusters.

Because each cluster was different—different individuals, situations, geographical locations, theological persuasions, and denominational loyalties—I customized the cluster content to the needs and situations of the participants and their congregations. The pastors determined the agenda, but the objective was to help each congregation in the cluster remove the specific blockage to fulfilling its ministry. Every pastor understood that he would be strictly accountable—not only to his board, spouse, and the Lord, but also to at least a half-dozen other pastors and an outside consultant. Every cluster member experienced a great spirit of excitement, commitment, and renewed anticipation of what God could do in his life, family, and ministry.

These experiences clarified that no matter what the denomination, part of the country, theological persuasion, situation and history of the church, or personality of the pastor— they all seemed to be working through very similar core issues in one way or another. This discovery led them to identify ten life-giving systems that comprised the essentials for revitalizing a church—ten critical points of ministry on which growing and healthy churches should focus. These life-giving systems are explored in this book.

To get the most from this book, it is suggested that each chapter be read in succession. You, the reader, however, may choose to scan the table of contents and go directly to a chapter that seems to hold the greatest interest for you as a church leader or member, and begin applying the ideas to your church. If you do so, it is recommended that you go back later and complete the remaining chapters. We hope that the interventions and strategies that are discussed will help pastors and congregations develop vibrant, healthy, and, most importantly, reproductive ministries.

A major premise of this book is that these lifesystems are interconnected and synergistic. Without understanding this concept, the reader might easily treat this book as another ten-steps-to-revitalization manual. This book proposes, however, that when all of the life-giving systems of a church are healthy and interlinked, they produce a vital interactive synergism that is greater than the whole, and that will help energize and revitalize your church.[14] Before looking, though, at the ten life-giving systems for revitalizing vibrant ministry, it will be useful to first read chapter 1. It considers some of the challenges that change is bringing to the church in the twenty-first century.

Questions to Consider

1. What recent changes in our world have made an impact on your church?
2. What challenges have these changes created?
3. What opportunities have they presented?
4. Are you taking advantage of the opportunities? Why or why not?

1

Societal Quakes Affecting the Twenty-First-Century Church

In the early 1970s, my (Dan's) family lived in France. My wife, Ethelwynne, and I had been sent to France to begin the work of the international Christian ministry of Campus Crusade for Christ. We were young and inexperienced in cross-cultural ministry. Ethelwynne had studied French in high school, but I couldn't speak a word of French.

We were living in a strange land, in a new culture, and had much to learn if we hoped to live there, let alone start a successful ministry to students and work with the French church. Learning the language was, of course, a high priority, as was becoming acquainted with the everyday life and thinking patterns of the people. We needed, for example, to get used to all businesses—stores, banks, and offices—closing down for two hours in the middle of the day. All of the employees and owners were at home or in a restaurant enjoying lunch and conversation. To "on-the-go" Americans, that was an adjustment, but we acclimatized.

Adjusting our lunchtime expectations, though, was minor. A greater challenge was sharing our faith in another language with people whose worldview was so different from ours. One time Ethelwynne was sharing her faith with some French students. She was pleased with the way it had gone until her fluent French-speaking companion let her know that by using the wrong article, *le,* instead of *la* with the French word for faith, *foi,* she had been talking about her liver instead of her faith!

These cultural and linguistic misunderstandings, although embarrassing and inconvenient, were far less consequential than those experienced in working with the French church. We learned a lesson about resistance to change, which is also an unfortunate characteristic of many people in American culture. The national ministry of Campus Crusade began to grow, and we now had teams that had been raised from both the work locally and new arrivals from the United States and Europe. We decided that the most effective way for our team to minister to the French church was for our team members to attend different churches in town.

Our family began attending a small congregation that met on the second floor of a commercial building about a mile from our home. There we learned valuable lessons in cross-cultural communication and the need for Christians to take into account the social realities and changes that surround all churches.

Originally, the church had been established by British and American missionaries but had long since become an entirely indigenous congregation. Its Sunday service was held at 10:30 a.m. and resembled, except for its being in French, a typical American or English service—hymns, Bible readings, an offering, announcements, and a sermon.

We soon discovered, however, that Sunday mornings in France are not like Sunday mornings in America. On Sunday mornings in Lyon, the streets for a mile around our apartment became a market. Vast crowds teemed at the market when it was time for the 10:30 a.m. church service to begin. Taking the car was out of the question, so we usually walked the mile through the market, slowed down by the crush of hundreds of busy shoppers and vendors. There we were, a group of Christians meeting at a time that was traditional for British and American churches, while the majority of French people were in the marketplace, many of them after having already attended Mass.

Being young and rash, I suggested to some of the church

leaders that they consider holding the worship service early in the morning, like the Catholic church did, and then go out into the marketplace to meet people, share the gospel, and invite people back to the church for a meal after the market was over. As you might guess, the idea did not go over well. Ten-thirty a.m. had become the "holy" hour, one at which real Christians in France would meet and separate themselves from those in the marketplace and those who attended Catholic churches in the early hours of the morning. A cultural tradition had become a badge of faith.

Societal Quakes

Moving into the twenty-first century, the church finds itself facing similar challenges. Communicating the gospel presents increasing cross-cultural issues, even in the United States.[1] Many churches find the cataclysmic changes of our day threatening and see change in the secular community as something that they must resist, even revile.[2] When churches finally do respond to societal changes, as most inevitably do, they often find themselves in the unfortunate position of being ten to fifteen years behind, introducing and promoting new approaches to ministry that are either no longer relevant, or are outmoded or even counterproductive.

It is not, of course, the mission of the church constantly to adapt and adjust to every societal fad. If, however, the church is not aware of what's happening in the lives and contexts of those it is called to reach with the gospel, it might find itself becoming unfaithful to Christ's Great Commission. What's the difference, though, between fads and, say, trends that indicate new but lasting changes? Fads are changes in which people are interested for a limited time. We often refer to fads as fashions, styles, or crazes. They're interesting but shouldn't set the agenda for the church. Trends, however, are changes that set new directions. The move, for example, toward hypercommunication via cell phones, Palm Pilots, e-mail, the Internet, and satellites is a trend, not a fad.

For more than 150 years following the invention of the telegraph in 1832 by Samuel F. B. Morse, telegrams were the national trend—a way of life for individuals and businesses. From the 1850s to the 1950s, many large companies, in fact, had their own telegraph offices. Yet hardly anyone receives telegrams anymore, which is not a fad, but a trend. Do not expect telegrams to make a comeback anytime soon.

So what are some of the societal shifts, or trends, that have occurred or are occurring that will influence how the church conducts itself and proclaims the biblical mission and message? We have identified seven shifts that nearly all churches face in the twenty-first century.

New Audiences

Ethelwynne, Dan's wife, teaches at a community college and frequently uses topical subjects as essay questions. One semester, she referred to Tom Brokaw's commentary on a current issue and asked her students to argue for or against the position. After reading the essays, she was amazed to find that more than two-thirds of the college students had no idea who Tom Brokaw was. They hadn't been watching NBC. Gary had a similar experience while teaching at Talbot School of Theology. During one class, he referred to the assassination of President John F. Kennedy and the impact it had on the people of the United States. To his shock, he discovered that most of the students in his class had no knowledge of John F. Kennedy.

If the church is to survive and thrive in the twenty-first century, it must respond to and communicate with multiple new audiences. Today's generations are being reared on MTV, video games, the Internet and other media. Modern young people have instant access to information, entertainment, and music via an increasing array of technological tools that are becoming as seamlessly integrated as has electricity into everyday life. The virtual reality generation has little interest in the past and a short attention span when it comes to the future. American communities no longer consist of a common culture, but multiple cultures abound. Groups and allegiances form around common assumptions, values, and beliefs that relegate people into segments and niches.

Because of these phenomena, such familiarities as TV programs can no longer be used as common reference points. Although some people might understand a reference to *Everybody Loves Raymond, Survivor,* or *Alias,* not everyone will have heard of these programs and even fewer will have actually watched them. But a couple of decades or so ago, a reference could be made to major network prime-time shows without any need to explain what it was because most people with television were watching them. Today, various populations are no longer watching the same programs. Futurists predict that hundreds, if not thousands, of programs will be available simultaneously. This means that, although media created a common culture in the last century, in the new one they will contribute to the fragmentation of a common culture. Now the strategic questions for churches concern which audiences they will target, what will best serve those audiences, and the communication channels that should be used.

> Today, various populations are no longer watching the same programs. Futurists predict that hundreds, if not thousands, of programs will be available simultaneously. This means that, although media created a common culture in the last century, in the new one they will contribute to the fragmentation of a common culture.

To find its own place in an era of diversity, a church will have to shift from a broad focus to a narrow focus. A target niche will not necessarily be governed by, as in the past, doctrinal nuances but by associations with groups with whom one resonates—maybe because of its worship, its vision, and its passion. Leaders of the last generation typically shied away from targeting specific audiences, taking instead a "one-size-fits-all" approach. Leaders in our new generations will need to be more sensitive to the specific group(s) of people they have chosen to reach and among whom to minister.

In an age when a person may change the channel with a push of a remote control button, the church must ensure both that it is not "preaching to the choir" but has the attention of its audience, and that people are listening and understanding. Since a common culture increasingly no longer exists, a local church should not try to be "all things to all people." Instead, each church must come alongside the culture in which it finds itself and become a redemptive community to "reach some of the people."

New Geographic and Size Values

During the coming years, a visible population shift will continue from suburban living to both "small town" life and urban living, and for similar reasons. After decades of preferring the tidy anonymity of the suburbs, people are, according to sociologists and demographers, developing a craving for community that small town life and urban neighborhoods afford. This almost unstoppable societal shift is observable in local driving patterns that reveal fewer people shop at huge malls halfway across the city. They are, instead, frequenting local main streets, business strips, one-stop "big box" stores, or smaller malls in convenient locations. There, consumers might be more familiar with store owners, and may enjoy more relaxed, authentic personal exchanges. In Southern California, developers are trying to capitalize on this trend by creating eclectic entertainment and shopping areas having courtyards, nonconforming architectural elements, and names such as "The Block." While megachurches will not go out of favor anytime soon, the future will witness a return to medium- and smaller-sized churches. This trend is already in process with multisite churches, the proliferation of house-church networks, and even churches that have no set geographical location. An August 2004 *Los Angeles Times* religion article reads,

> The one-year-old church in Orange County has no
> name, no building and no set time to meet. . . .
> Shepherded by Spencer Burke, a former pastor at the
> 10,000-member Mariners Church in Irvine, a small band
> of men and women belong to this highly movable
> congregation.[3]

Size and location of church are not as important as they used
to be, a trend that could cause a lot of consternation in church
board rooms. Many church leaders and consultants, however,
see that in the near future the optimum size for the typical church
is about three hundred to five hundred people. The emphasis,
though, will be on community, authenticity, and a move away
from the primacy of buildings.

New Identities and Affiliations

Although the trend to smaller churches may have arrived, these
churches and groups will continue to be connected and affiliated with like-minded groups, but not necessarily along denominational lines. In our global, heterogeneous world, it is more likely
that "tribal" allegiances will develop, supplanting denominational
loyalties and organizational affiliations. I (Dan) facilitate the
Council on Ecclesiology, the mission of which is to lend unity
and clarity on the nature, function, and mission of the church to
evangelical churches, and to influence them in constructive ways
during a time of enormous theological confusion. The Council
also encourages evangelical churches to adequately reflect on both
theology and missiology in relation to their traditional and contemporary expressions. The most important ecclesiological question now for unity is not to what denomination a church or a
person belongs but with whom (tribe, movement, or association) one primarily identifies.

The core principles of even significant megachurches such as
Willow Creek and Saddleback evoke concepts rather than
ecclesial connections. For some churches, being a "purpose-

driven" church is more important to their identity than denominational affiliation. Such is the case in regard to Erwin McManus's "Mosaic" or Wayne Cordeiro's "New Hope." Informal affiliations and associations have formed around such churches because people want to be "in the orbit" of meaningful ministry and to feel a resonance with the heart of a ministry. These "tribes" cut across denominational and institutional lines. Although each may have a different emphasis, ethos, and distinctive, none are institutionally rule bound. Rather, they are mission and vision driven, and seek biblical responses to a complex post-Christian world.

Likewise, people who are seeking a church with which to be affiliated are less likely to make their choices based on denominational labels. Whereas once, people arriving in town or those wanting to start attending church might have made their decision based on a denominational affiliation or memory, today most people who are looking for a church are doing so for many different reasons. Further, those who are not looking for a church do not understand the meaning of such labels as Evangelical Free Church, First Missionary Baptist Church, or Orthodox Presbyterian, much less some of the other labels we give churches—Church of the Master, Living Water Church, or Little Church in the Valley.

New Communication and Delivery Systems

New ways of communicating and receiving information are at the heart of the changes the church must address as it moves into the twenty-first century. Multidimensional, multisensory images are now more compelling, effective, and accessible than one-dimensional print. The move to visual communication via video, DVD, and projected images is a trend that will continue in churches for the foreseeable future.

Sequential thinking, too, is gradually being replaced by nonsequential thinking. This trend in emphasis from left-brained, sequential thinking to a more creative, artistic right-brained focus favors a greater emphasis on the experiential and spiritual. Indeed, for churches seeking to reach today's new audiences, structured, three-point sermons may not be the best way to communicate. Instead, using narrative, drama, or visual approaches may be more effective in communicating spiritual truths.

Another quake the church must acknowledge is the change in the educational delivery system. Collaborative and cooperative learning, attention to diversity in learning styles, and integration of disciplines are trends in education. The lecture format, perpetuated by the learning style of the academic community, is giving way to interactive teaching, or what some people refer to as "learner centered" or "active learning." In addition, diminishing financial resources and an increase in the population to be served have caused serious revisions of educational strategy and delivery. These trends correlate with the other trends already noted, and they also will affect the way in which the church delivers theological and practical education.

For meeting the training needs of church leaders, traditional educational institutions and denominations are being perceived as less effective than in the past. In their place are emerging a wide range of creative methodologies for equipping prospective leaders with skills and strategies for new audiences. Seminars and training given by effective pastors will also generate higher participation than the theoretical approaches offered by academic scholars. The whole concept of separating knowledge from practice is, in fact, being questioned, and this growing demand for hands-on training in the nuts and bolts of ministry will continue. On-the-job education through mentoring, either individually or in groups by consultants or other specialists, will be a viable option for many practicing church leaders. Because delaying careers or leaving home is less desirable (impossible for many people), the classroom will be brought to the student through a variety of means such as interactive broadcasts and the Internet. All of these new training associations and affiliations will play an increasingly greater role in educating people for ministry, and some of the more established churches, such as

Willow Creek, already have many of these techniques in motion, especially in the area of continuing education.

New Methods

As a means of getting people involved in society in general, one quake recently at work is a shift from programs and events to grassroots movements and networks. This phenomenon is evident in political campaigns in which people vote for candidates on personal recommendations rather than by party allegiance. Millions of dollars are often collected through networks and grassroots efforts, which was seen in the presidential campaigns of Ross Perot and, more recently, Howard Dean.

A parallel rise is observed in churches in the disenchantment with conventional programming as a means of attracting and holding newcomers. People tend to select churches on the basis of personal recommendation rather than by denominational affiliation. Newcomers desire to be part of a group or network that meets their needs for community. They shy away from formal programming that does not connect with them. Whereas committed church members used to be in church "every time the doors are open," now even the committed people do not see being involved in everything as a sign of their commitment, and they choose relational connection and projects over programs. This change also affects giving. The concerns and passions of an individual's peer group and community connections, rather than traditional fundraising appeals and programs, tend to determine where members invest their money.

New Structures

Organizational structures are evolving to deal with a rapidly changing world. Trends in private industry emphasize the flattening of administration, the creation of fluid teams to meet changing needs, and the embedding at all levels of responsibility, accountability, and authority. New theories of management tend to shy away from organizational charts and job descriptions that represent a top-down structure in which tasks are delegated downward and authority is tightly held and micromanaged. Emerging structures look like an inverted triangle in which structure and job descriptions are constructed with an emphasis on supporting the accomplishment of work rather than monitoring and controlling.

Churches that adjust appropriately to this trend place less emphasis on controlling, monitoring, and reporting. Instead, they place more emphasis on decentralization and empowerment. This change in emphasis results in what might be called a "release" of new leaders and teams. When bureaucracies control agendas, ministry is stifled. More leaders are developed, however, and more ministry occurs where permissions are given and authority is released, allowing emerging leaders to experiment with new forms of ministry. The critical ingredient in releasing new leaders and teams is trust. When there is trust, sharing and owning of vision, when leadership empowerment and reporting is relational and informal, there is room for healthful growth.

New Fears

Finally, the shadow that September 11, 2001, cast across this country has presented us all with a new reality. No one will ever be the same. We live in a radically changed world in which some people seek a safe haven from the new dangers that confront us all, and in which others want to be "dangerous" in combating the new threats. This point also applies to the church, in which are those who seek to provide stability to believers, connect with past traditions, and provide a place "within the walls" of the church that is the safest place on earth. Others have become aggressively focused externally and predict that being Christians in the next few decades is a dangerous proposition. These more aggressive Christians suggest, therefore, that we should get used to being "dangerous"—that is, realistic, compelling, and less comfortable. They remind us that in the early days of the church, as well as throughout history, to be a Christian was very dangerous and that many Christians paid with their lives.

Questions About Quakes

These societal shifts raise questions about their impact. How will these changes, and others that will come, look when they are combined? Will they be similar to or different from what has gone before? We are not advocating a frenetic overhaul of everything that is going on in your church. Some aspects of ministry will look virtually the same. We advocate, though, a change in the way you see and think about the world. Consider those who do not attend church. The way they see and think about the world has changed dramatically.

Some pastors have practical questions about how change can occur in their particular church. One pastor put it thus:

> This quake you describe may very well be true. I have been reading about it for some time and I have been talking about it today. But what do I do about it? If I were to go back and advocate change to my congregation, I would be out of a job tomorrow. This is because those to whom I minister are not ready to hear this. They do not like change.

Most pastors have a similar sense of what is realistic for their congregations. They understand that most concepts involving change are often too radical for most church members.

Pastors who wish to address the quakes taking place and equip their churches to respond to them must remember two things. First, people evince different rates at which they adapt to and adopt change—whether it be microwave ovens or contemporary worship services. Some people are early adopters, eager to adopt any kind of change, becoming convinced quickly and wanting to introduce innovations immediately. Most people, however, are middle adopters, perhaps taking several years of convincing—with frequent reinforcement. A few people are late adopters, and some people never adopt change. Church leaders will be disappointed if they assume that their congregations will understand instantly and accept change simply because the need has been explained and clearly demonstrated.

Second, it is important to understand people's differing generational perspectives. Each generation marches to a different drummer, and its members might have significantly different perspectives of the world. We must listen to individual beats and be culturally sensitive so that we can better communicate spiritual truth.

Despite these provisos, it is not necessary to shy away from addressing rapidly changing realities. Rather, it is appropriate to ask one's self how to be, as Paul said long ago, "all things to all people, so that we can win some."

Questions to Consider

1. Have the societal quakes discussed in this chapter affected your church? If so, what have been the repercussions?
2. How aware of these quakes are your leaders?
3. How aware is your congregation?
4. What major challenges do these quakes create for your church's ministry?

Toxic Terrain, Hot Air Balloons, and Spinning Plates

Three images or metaphors come to mind when thinking about what is typically restricting a church from healthy growth. First is the image of a toxic dump. You might say that's a little harsh. It is—but numerous books have been written and studies conducted showing that institutions and individuals are held back by their history—the "baggage" they're carrying and the patterns they've established in the past—and this can result in a toxic environment. The second image is a hot air balloon. It provides the most accurate picture of how life systems relate to identifying and overcoming specific obstacles to revitalization. The third image is of spinning plates—an image that has often been used to symbolize being overloaded, of one person doing it all himself or herself, doing more and achieving less. What are some of the restrictive conditions in churches that these images describe?

Toxic Terrain

Bill was a successful business owner who was very active in his small local church. He'd been a board member for longer than most people could remember. In the fifteen years since the inception of the church, Bill had served faithfully as the chairperson of the pastoral search committee for five different pastors. He and his family had been among the founders of the church, which began as a split from another church in town. The reason for the split, according to Bill and the other founding members, was that the pastor of their former church introduced unbiblical ideas into the church. Bill gave very generously to his church; neither the new hymnals nor the organ would have been possible without his financial support.

Despite the commitment of people like Bill, however, none of the five pastors was able to help the church grow, and many of them had not stayed much longer than a year. Their reasons for leaving always seemed plausible, and their departures were always cordial and uneventful. Although Bill was well known for his generosity and commitment, less known was that, behind the scenes, Bill had controlled all five of the church's pastors. Every decision that was made, regardless of whether he was involved, had to be approved by him. He had even met with two of the younger pastors to "help" them develop sermon ideas. Bill was, in fact, the unseen but real leader of the church. The church began to revitalize its ministry only when this unhealthful pattern was acknowledged and addressed.

Eight years ago, John, the pastor of a midsized congregation in California, began to feel distressed and discouraged. One Thursday evening, after the choir had finished its rehearsal, he got into a conversation with Joan, one of the choir members. Finding that their conversation was taking longer than expected, they adjourned to a nearby coffee shop after everyone else had gone home. During the course of their conversation, John shared some inappropriate information with Joan concerning another member of the church. The next day, John called Joan and together they agreed that the conversation had not been edifying and that they would put it behind them. Although the incident was buried for a time, it was uncovered recently during a conversation Joan had with a disgruntled member of the church. The wife of an attorney, the member used the information to cause major damage in the church.

Figure 2.1

In both of these stories, which are based on actual cases, the effectiveness of both the church and the pastor was diminished, thwarted, and undermined by toxic conditions that were part of the history of the church. A complete health checkup of the life-giving systems of most congregations will likely result in sobering realities. Unhealthy congregations often have toxic antibodies, which create unhealthful conditions that attack the lifesystems of the church. Pastors of such churches often are left wondering what it will take to rid the church body of this toxicity and restore the church to health. Where should they begin? In some situations, the entire ministry will need surgery. Band-Aids cannot remedy the internal conditions.

Often a health checkup or analysis must be conducted and all of the critical life-giving systems checked. Key health tests must be run, using not only standard surveys—in which key issues are often missed—but also by examining and analyzing the human element. Some life-giving systems will pass the tests, but others will not. All areas will eventually need to be restored to health, usually beginning with the most serious areas first.

Hot Air Balloons

To change the metaphor, another way of looking at the process of revitalization is to imagine the church as a colorful hot air balloon. Ballooning is very popular in certain geographic areas of the country. Some people find no better way to view the spectacular scenery than from a thousand feet up at sunrise, as I (Dan) discovered on my one (and only) balloon ride in Napa Valley, California. I discovered, however, that certain conditions are necessary if the balloon is to rise off the ground and soar into the sky.

Figure 2.2

Condition 1: All of the Ropes Must Be Removed

A balloon may be colorful and attractive, its pilot confident and experienced, but if the ropes holding the balloon to the ground are not removed, it won't be able to rise into the sky. In a church setting, it is important to identify what is holding the ministry back—that is, keeping it tethered.

In one Kansas church, a crowded, unattractive nursery was keeping the ministry tied down. Parents were reluctant to leave their infants in the overcrowded nursery; it affected their desire to attend the church. Visitors with very young children often found the unattractive nursery sufficient reason not to return to the church. When the church finally paid attention to this aspect of its ministry, they relocated, refurbished, repurposed, and re-staffed their nursery, making it bright, attractive, and welcoming. With that rope removed, a vital ministry to newborns and their parents has developed, and the church has been able to reach out to the many young families in their neighborhood. Visitors with young children tend to stay, and many church members are happily using their gifts in a ministry that is tied to the vision and direction of the church.

Condition 2: Extra Weight Must Be Removed

Excess weight will keep a hot air balloon grounded. Even if all the ropes are released, if too much ballast is aboard the balloon it will stagger across the ground instead of lifting off. Similarly, a church will not be able to soar if it is carrying excess weight.

Excess weight occasionally is found in the spiritual dynamics of a church. For example, in a young, vibrant Texas congregation, two members of the pastoral staff engaged in serious conflict. Even though both staff members had tremendous potential and the church was ready to move forward, the entire church found itself weighted down with depression. After the conflict was mediated, one of the pastors found ministry elsewhere, and the ministry was able to lift off effectively once again.

Additional weight frequently comes in the form of a program that has outlived its usefulness. Most church programs and projects start in response to a need or as part of a clearly articulated vision. Years later, however, the need may no longer exist or the vision has changed. Yet the program chugs on, expending energy and time, resisting discontinuation because it's something the church has always done.[1] One church, for example, had run a hugely successful elementary school on its premises. During the school's first decade, it paid its way financially and brought many new families into contact with the church. Circumstances changed as the school progressed through its second decade. It gradually became harder for the school to meet its financial obligations, enrollment fell, and staff members were let go. The church eventually found itself subsidizing the school each successive year. Instead of being a blessing, the school became a burden. Because the school had been a part of the church's past vision, many people were reluctant to give it up. Only when members of the congregation were able to cast a new vision of their ministry and understand that a Christian school was not part of their mission did the church remove the excess weight and achieve liftoff.

Condition 3: New Blasts of Energy Must Be Released

When the ropes are released and the weight is reduced, a balloon will not rise into the air until several blasts of heat are released into the balloon. The power that raised Christ from the grave is available to the church, but in some cases pastors and congregations ignore the source of energy and focus on doing business as usual. When a church is focused and intent on tapping God's power, and obeying his command to make disciples, liftoff will take place.

A charismatic church in Colorado was struggling in regard to organization and administration. It had able pastors and leaders, but they were overworked and bogged down with administrative detail. Several intercessors became serious about focusing their prayers, like laser beams, on the need of the church for an able administrator. Within several months, by obvious divine orchestration, a businessman who had taken early retirement filled their need. His work energized the overworked pastor and youth leader, and his ministry enabled the church to focus more resources on its mission.

Through the vision of three or four of its members, a mainline church in Missouri designed a new worship service to reach the community around the church. A talented saxophone player volunteered to play, and the worship service was built around his jazz-flavored style of music. Soon, a regular crowd was attending and bringing their friends, many of whom had never entered a church before. As a result, many people heard the gospel for the first time, small-group Bible studies were initiated to meet the needs of the new seekers, and the church began to grow.

In both of the above situations, bursts of energy helped each church reach new ministry heights.

In hot air ballooning, it takes only the removal of one rope, one weight, and one blast of hot air to start it rising off the ground. As other ropes, weights, and blasts are released, a critical point is reached. Once enough obstacles are removed and sufficient energy is released, natural laws take over. The balloon can no longer remain on the ground. It takes off!

A remarkably similar phenomenon occurs in churches that need revitalization. Liftoff begins when new spiritual energy in the form of prayer or vision is blasted into a stagnated congregation. The energy continues as a church prayerfully identifies what is holding them back, intentionally cuts the ropes, and throws out the excess baggage. As ropes and weights are removed and spiritual life is injected, the critical point of liftoff inevitably will occur. In most instances, two to five years of intentional "removal and releasing" activities must be invested before a lasting and measurable reversal of trends can be observed, and the church can begin to soar.[2]

Spinning Plates

Many years ago on a trip to New Orleans, I (Dan) was delighted to stumble upon a seasoned juggler on an open-air stage surrounded by a rapt crowd. The juggler's most suspenseful routine involved a dozen plates that he spun one by one on top of freestanding wooden poles. Each time a plate would begin to wobble, nearly crashing to the ground, the juggler started it spinning again. With admirable dexterity, he darted from plate to plate, keeping them all spinning at once. Volunteers were soon asked to duplicate the feat. No one in the crowd could get more than one or two spinning at one time. Plates were crashing constantly amid the shrieks of the bystanders.

If ever imagery described the challenge of everyday church ministry, this is it! In interviews with pastors over the past twenty years, we have heard countless stories of struggle to keep all of the plates spinning. Many pastors experience a perpetual feeling of never quite keeping up and of finding no practical way to avoid periodic crashes. The typical pastor of a small- to medium-sized church has to teach, preach, lead worship, administer the affairs of the church, and offer counsel. The list of ministry activities goes on and on.

Recently, a pastor was grappling with the consequences of needing to spin more plates if his church was to grow. He said, "Why would I want my church to grow from 150 to 450 in the next three years? I'm already working harder than I should. My wife is complaining that I'm never with the family, and I'm dropping plates all over the place. There's no more of me left for growth."

Figure 2.3

We have found that many pastors and church leaders feel the same way. They are not settled, focused, or fruitful. Some pastors display multiple symptoms of ministry burnout and are a bottleneck for growth. The consequences are costly.

The alternative to spinning plates is to find committed and qualified individuals who can come alongside the pastor to form a leadership team. Each member of the team concentrates on keeping one plate spinning, and the pastor and other leaders are freed to spin a maximum of only two or three plates. In this way, the ministry is supported by many rather than a few.[3] As will be seen in later chapters, focusing on the essential areas of ministry and developing a strategy to restore a church's life-giving systems to health will make a major difference. One of the major life-giving systems involves having the right people doing the right things at the right times in the right places.

Synergism Is the Secret

As the illustrations of the hot air balloon and the spinning plates emphasize, the correction of just one problem or the introduction of one visionary idea is not the answer to revitalizing a church. Rather, the answer is the interaction of all the parts. As a congregation majors on the majors and is not distracted by peripheral issues, the effect is synergistic. When enough of the life-giving systems become healthy, there is a critical movement. Positive forces take charge over negative ones. When this occurs, the church will lift off, just like the hot air balloon. But what are the parts that work synergistically? They are the ten life-giving systems.

Some time ago, I (Dan) went to my doctor for a routine checkup and was surprised to find out that I had outrageously elevated cholesterol levels. The doctor's analysis came as a shock because years earlier I'd altered my diet and lifestyle habits. My family had switched to low-fat milk; we had all but eliminated fatty snacks, desserts, and fried foods. In addition, I was physically active, swimming seriously at least twice a week. Yet the warning signs were there, and they called for more than casual attention; they called for intentional focus and action. So I began to follow a very strict regimen and within three months was able to significantly reduce the cholesterol levels. It required discipline and an intentional approach to dealing with a potentially life-threatening situation.

As recently as thirty years ago, controlling cholesterol was not recognized as an essential ingredient to maintaining health and preventing untimely death. Today, technological advances enable us to be aware of the cholesterol factor and be intentional in our actions so we can enjoy good health. Any reasonable person would agree that if we can detect a problem in our body's vital systems, we'd do so. Any reasonable person would further agree to be attentive to the corrective prescriptions or reasonable regimens to promote health and well-being. That some people do not, and suffer the consequences, does not negate this principle.

Likewise, churches that desire to experience healthy growth must focus intentionally on those factors of congregational life that are essential for their growth. Some, perhaps most, churches are "coincidental" in their thinking rather than intentional. They have a fuzzy focus and a haphazard approach to church life and mission. Perhaps they think that they'll remain healthy as long as they keep on keeping on. As has been seen, however, churches must actively face societal changes and deal with toxicity, obstacles, and weight if they are to maintain an energetic and vital focus on the mission of God. A church cannot ignore its vital signs any more than a person can ignore the signs of cholesterol. Healthy churches take seriously the signs coming from their life-giving systems and chart a course toward continued health and vitality.

To prepare your congregation for vibrant ministry, it's important to identify and understand the critical health factors and where changes must be made. Four critical points must be kept in balance if a church is to chart a future course toward robust ministry. Within each of these four points are various life-giving systems, which, in a healthy church, function together and support one another, producing vitality in the church body. These life-giving systems are not programs; instead, each represents an important element, a prescription if you will, for recovery from stagnation.

For some churches, restoring these basic life-giving systems to ultimate health means the difference between death and survival. For congregations that are currently experiencing growth, improving these life-giving systems will ensure continued reproductive health under each of the four critical points.

Critical Point A: Generating Spiritual Energy
Life-Giving System 1: Pastor's Spiritual Life
Life-Giving System 2: Corporate Intercession
Life-Giving System 3: Spiritual Disciplines

Critical Point B: Developing Effective Leaders
Life-Giving System 4: Mentoring Relationships
Life-Giving System 5: Team Ministry

Critical Point C: Increasing People Flow
Life-Giving System 6: People-Flow Strategy
Life-Giving System 7: Lifestyle Evangelism

Critical Point D: Charting Amid Change
Life-Giving System 8: Charting the Future
Life-Giving System 9: Streamlining the Organization
Life-Giving System 10: Thriving on Change

The following chapters explain these life-giving systems. They work together to help a church engage the various societal shifts in a healthful manner, and work through any of the inhibiting factors a church may find in place. Your church *can* build healthful life-giving systems and retrofit itself for future ministry.

Questions to Consider

1. Do any unhealthful, toxic situations exist in your church that need to be addressed? What are they?
2. Do any ropes or excess weight need to be removed? What are they?
3. Are pastors and leaders spinning too many plates? If so, what plates are dropping?
4. What new blasts of energy are waiting to be released in your church before it can lift off in renewed ministry?

3

Life-Giving System 1: Pastor's Spiritual Life

A few years ago, I (Gary) was consulting with a church on the East Coast. On the surface, the life-giving systems of the church seemed to be fairly healthy. Upon closer inspection, however, it became clear that the spiritual energy of the church was lacking. The atmosphere, particularly during the two Sunday morning worship services, depressed rather than uplifted the congregation.

During a number of the interviews conducted by my team over the weekend, several people mentioned concerns regarding the worship pastor. Further investigation revealed that ten months before the consulting visit, the worship pastor had become angry with a group of people in the church. Instead of dealing with the conflict proactively, however, the worship pastor internalized his anger and chose to ignore them. Over the ensuing months, members of the congregation noticed that the worship pastor had made the unfortunate decision not to speak to any of the people who were involved in the conflict. If he met one of them in the church's hallways, for example, he would look away and walk past the person without speaking. On social occasions, he refused to sit at the same table with some of these same members. According to the people interviewed during the consulting visit, the worship pastor had refused to speak to some members of the church for nearly ten months!

While this conflict directly involved only a very few people in the church, it affected the entire church. Nearly every member of the congregation was aware that the pastor who led them in worship each Sunday was not speaking to some people in the church. The spiritual energy of the church sank to an all-time low. The congregation could not enthusiastically participate in worship that was led by a pastor who obviously had some spiritual issues in his life. Each Sunday members of the congregation found themselves looking into the face of a worship pastor whom they knew was not walking his talk. The inability of the worship leader to come to grips with his spiritual issues—and the lack of mentors and friends to help him do that—was draining the church's spiritual energy.

Our consulting team doesn't often come across this extreme, obvious, and ongoing spiritual sabotage. The example illustrates, however, the importance of the spiritual life of church pastors and leaders to the health and growth of the church. External factors can, indeed, cause a church to die or not to grow, but regardless of the state of a church's overall health, the state of the pastors' and leaders' spiritual life is, without question, the most important single reason why some churches are growing and others are declining in numbers. Indeed, for the vast majority of churches, spiritual dynamics are the principal factor for growth and health. Where churches are growing, spiritual energy is being generated, and the energy occurs primarily when three essential life-giving systems—"heart allegiance" of the pastors and leaders, corporate prayer, and spiritual disciplines—are well and functioning.

Research has shown that no institutional factor is more significant to the overall growth patterns of churches than the effectiveness of pastoral leadership.[1] Dan and I believe that nothing is more important to the lasting effectiveness of ministry than a leader's intentional focus on a *vital* spiritual life. Yes, it's important that a leader's style and gifts be appropriate for a given church body, but vision, education, spiritual gifts, or the amount of ministry experience cannot equal, in long-term impact, the quality of a burning and broken heart—that is, the quality of *heart allegiance*. Numerous terms are very close in meaning to *heart allegiance*, but no single term includes all that the term means. Some alternative terms are, for example, *surrendered, submitted, humble, broken, Christ-controlled, crucified, captivated,* or *authentic*.

King David's life demonstrates the balance that God desires in every leader's life. Psalm 78:72 states, "So he [David] shepherded them according to the integrity of his heart, and guided them with his skillful hands." Heart and hands, character and competence—however we say it, the need for synergy and balance in this area is evident. To be a spiritual leader demands a passionate heart allegiance toward God. It's no mistake that the psalmist mentions first the *integrity* of David's heart. The word *integrity* means literally "simplicity" and points out that David simply wanted God to be first in his life. It does not mean that David was perfect or without sin, a fact that we all recognize. David's simplicity of heart did, however, lead him to repent of sin whenever it invaded his life. He was captivated by God and broken and humble before Him. It's true that David was competent, leading Israel with skillful hands, but his strategic success was undergirded by his character of spiritual integrity. Similarly, our pastoral leaders need both "heart" and "hands," "character" and "competence"; integrity of heart, though, must come first. A great deal is at stake, because heart allegiance is not only personally essential for church leaders but also prerequisite for forward ministry momentum. *Whether a ministry succeeds or fails over the long haul depends, to a large extent, on what is going on in the secret spiritual compartments of a pastor's life.*

Whether a ministry succeeds or fails over the long haul depends, to a large extent, on what is going on in the secret spiritual compartments of a pastor's life.

Attitude Makes the Difference

A good friend of mine (Gary's) has a personal license plate on his car that reads "ADA 2UD." It is his way of communicating to those around him that attitude makes a profound difference in our actions—spiritual or natural. Attitude, though, can sometimes be faked. Some actors, for example, show a great attitude when on stage in front of the curtain, but when they step off stage and go behind the curtain, their attitudes and actions change dramatically. The lack of a consistent attitude between being in front of or behind the curtain results in often shocking, unexpected actions.

Church consultant Kent Hunter reminds us, "Pilots speak of the attitude of an airplane. It is the angle of the nose of the airplane. The attitude affects all the other systems of the airplane."[2] If the nose of the plane points up, the plane goes up; if it points down, the plane goes down. Likewise, the spiritual attitude of a church's pastor or pastors affects all the other life-giving systems in the church.

Boards and congregations often take for granted the spiritual attitude of a pastor's life and experience. They assume that healthy ones come with the diploma or ordination papers, and they see little reason to be concerned about, or to question, the spiritual life of the pastor—unless something goes drastically wrong. The assumption is that the pastor knows how to handle spiritual development without any assistance. As a spiritual leader, the pastor is supposed to be responsible for the spiritual needs of others.

As we begin a consultation with a church, however—and despite what we may have seen and heard about a particular minister—we never "assume" that his or her spiritual life is adequate or in order. We've learned not to wait for the subject to come up and, as a rule, we ask about it during our very first interview. In my (Dan's) ministry among clusters of pastors, I make this subject my primary focus during the first few hours we're together.

During nearly three decades of ministry, we have observed that pastors face common barriers to their spiritual growth and development.

Ministry Overextension

To our personal knowledge, the number of pastors who have left ministry because of overextension is alarming. The number of persons to whom a pastor provides close attention—that is, his or her span of care—is at optimum five to seven people. An overextended pastor has double or triple that span of care. As pastors attempt to meet unrealistic expectations, they begin spinning too many plates. They're fearful of releasing responsibilities to others, whom they fear will drop one of the plates. It's a vicious cycle—pastors come to believe that if anything is to happen, it's up to them to make it happen, and they focus on tasks rather than ministry. In many cases, however, none of the plates they're spinning is their own personal spiritual growth and intimacy with God and others. Years ago I (Dan) began consultations focusing on leaders' spiritual lives, and one of the biggest surprises for me was how few of them read the Bible outside their sermon preparation. Their own personal devotions were practically nonexistent; it had been squeezed out of their lives by their heavy workload.

It is with unfortunate ease that church leaders capitulate to the corporate mode, which emphasizes a command-and-control structure and organizational efficiency. Leaders need to learn how they can shift into a mission-team mode. Many leaders and pastors find it difficult, however, to take this plunge because they often haven't operated outside of their comfort zone, forced to depend completely and constantly on God. In a surprising number of cases, we also find that many leaders have never had to relate at a deep level to other persons, which is essential in today's team environment.

Lack of Transparency

Assessing someone's spiritual life is often difficult because of its subjective and personal nature. The congregation usually does not consider the health of the pastor's private spiritual life their concern or responsibility. Thus, their response to the pastor's spiritual life is WYSIWYG ("What you see is what you get"). But, like so many of us, pastors are good at behaving in a way that's expected of them. It can be difficult for church members and leaders to determine if their pastor's spirituality is not as it should be. How can members and leaders know, for example, that what pastors say is true? How can a pastor's spirituality be measured and validated? In addition, churches often lack a culture in which it is safe for pastors to be open about their own spiritual struggles and victories.

Few Close Relationships

This unfortunate situation is exacerbated by pastors' having few, if any, close relationships. As a result, pastors may have no one with whom they can share or discuss their own spiritual lives, especially if they have struggles. Just as some doctors excel at prescribing and treating the illnesses of their patients but find little time to take care of their own health needs, pastors find it easy to get overloaded and busy with the work of the church, neglecting or failing to nurture their own spiritual lives. Pastors do well when the curtain opens and they step out front to "do" ministry in front of others. But when the curtain closes and they step behind it into their private worlds, they often are less successful.

The difference between what happens in front of the curtain and what happens behind the curtain is one test of church health. In the healthiest of churches we find a high degree of consistency between the behavior of leaders and leadership teams in front of and behind the curtain. Where major inconsistency in behavior is evident between the front and back of the curtain, forward momentum in the church will not be sustainable for more than a brief period of time and the health of the church will begin to deteriorate. This deterioration, resulting from lack of pastoral accountability in open and honest relationships, will become evident. That deterioration eventually will also become apparent to those outside the inner circle and, perhaps more significantly, to those outside of the church and the faith.[3]

A New Revolution

During the 1980s and 1990s, churches gradually adopted the practices of the corporate world. In far too many congregations excellent ministry practice was often valued more than godliness. These two qualities are not, of course, mutually exclusive. Nevertheless, without developing adequate safeguards, excellence can often become the dominant aim. Without a strong emphasis on personal discipleship and spiritual disciplines, pastors and congregations will drift inevitably into stagnation and lifeless institutionalism.

During the past decades, though, developing personal relationships has not always been encouraged. Pastors and other church leaders have often been able to hide behind successful programs. As long as the personal needs of attendees were being met, troubles among pastoral staff were either unnoticed or seemed inconsequential, just part of the normal working environment.

In recent years, a revolution has been occurring. Authentic and contagious personal relationships are now seen as essential to ministry fruitfulness. The current wave is taking us back to our roots in the first-century church. Visionary and innovative pioneers, such as Wayne Cordeiro of New Hope Church, O'ahu, and Erwin McManus of Mosaic Church in metropolitan Los Angeles, are pointing the way to a more promising ancient/future church. New Hope and Mosaic, although birthed in quite different denominations and locations, are two emerging laboratories that have reached similar conclusions on how the church will look and operate in our rapidly changing world. New Hope discovered these insights—discussed below—as a rapid church plant. Mosaic reached similar conclusions in the midst of redeveloping a plateaued congregation. Each of them looks more like a missionary movement than what Americans have generally defined as a conventional church.

The radiance and zeal of the exceptional leaders of these churches and their leadership teams clearly can be traced to what goes on behind the curtain. Both pastors model a humble, sacrificial, and disciplined life. Leadership teams perceive themselves as servants in a global cause rather than as members who exist to maintain an institution. Both of these radical Christian communities have placed a higher priority on developing authentic relationships than on maintaining and running programs. Both of them have learned how to form and rapidly reproduce discipleship teams that see discipleship as "going and growing" and "making and reproducing disciples," as distinct from churches that emphasize more structured education and formation programs. Churches such as New Hope and Mosaic confirm what we have sensed for a long time: spiritual energy rises and spreads throughout congregations when pastors pour their lives into a few carefully selected leaders.

In both settings, the spiritual lives of the leaders are open for all to see. In New Hope, for example, one of the main qualifications for leadership (if not the only one) is "the journal," a daily Bible-reading plan and personal meeting with God in His Word. It consists of reading passages from the Old and New Testaments (doing this daily for a year results in reading the Old Testament once and the New Testament twice), recording the Scripture, observation, application, a prayer, and asking, "How will I be different today because of what I have just read?" (The journal is discussed in more detail in case study 6.) All over Honolulu on any given day, members of the ten-thousand-member church, including Wayne Cordeiro, are seen in coffee shops reading their Bibles and journaling. They share what they've learned with each other in teams and at home, and have something from God's

Word to share with people who need it, whom they meet along the way.

Throughout America, congregations are emerging with similar patterns of relational and reproductive team ministry. Missional teams—that is, teams that are mission focused—provide the optimum context for generating spiritual energy because they ignite creative sparks between individuals—including the pastor—who were previously operating in isolation. Missional teams enable Christians to morph from a stagnant facade to a revolutionary force with the eventual capacity to transform entire cities. Missional teams enable Christians from diverse backgrounds and differing perspectives to coalesce as a team rather than spin apart.

The spiritual lives of pastors and missional team leaders are formed increasingly by interactive approaches, rather than in settings with conventional teaching and preaching. Similarly, more and more congregations are discovering that the spiritual lives of their leaders are developed more significantly, becoming what Tom Bandy describes as *a church in motion rather than a church at rest.*[4]

Whole new sets of skills—skill sets—for spiritual development are replacing the more program-based approaches of the last generation. Leaders are developing communities in which relational skills and emotional intelligence can be used and developed alongside and interacting with skills that are task oriented and strategy driven. These churches realize the interdependency of people and their skills as Christians work together toward mission. All Christians have, of course, personal goals and desires. But interaction with one another in these authentic missional communities results in a synergism from "iron sharpening iron." This synergy helps propel the mission forward and provides energy, motivation, and magnetism in those who are involved.

The "one another" passages of Scripture are often overlooked when the emphasis is on individual classroom development. The "all-for-one-and-one-for-all" attitudes, though, are once again becoming a priority. Christians are discovering that one plus one often equals four or five rather than two. As Scripture records, "And if one can overpower him who is alone, two can resist him. A cord of three strands is not quickly torn apart" (Eccl. 4:12). A new wave of ministry is appearing in which spiritual lives are more radical and contagious, and complacency is being replaced by serving others sacrificially.

Another encouraging discovery is that early detection of and preventative measures in regard to spiritual decay can transform ministers before some irreversible calamity occurs. We've all grieved when some of God's most effective servants commit private sins that have made sensational headlines. Each time I (Dan) read of another instance, my heart sinks, I cry uncontrollably, and my anger erupts with outbursts: "You fool! How could you?" Then, almost instantly, I hear a voice that reminds me, "But for My grace, this would be you!" Experience tells us that these events took years to produce, and the gradual and unmonitored erosion of personal, intimate spiritual connections was a contributing factor.

Most congregational members are unaware when their pastors or their pastors' spouses are facing serious difficulties and are on the path to burnout. In our opinion, the number of severe cases has been underreported. The pressure is especially difficult for pastors' spouses, who often feel trapped and do not have a safe place to receive care.

During the past decade, I've worked with scores of pastoral couples, in a LifeMapping process. This process helps them in times of personal and vocational decision or crisis to gain perspective for the next part of their journeys. In these two- or three-day private consultations, husbands and wives are able to take time away from their children and the heavy burdens of pastoral ministry to meet in pleasant and peaceful surroundings. There, they gain a much clearer perspective on their relationships and ministry.

As I listen to each of them describe their personal journeys; turning points in faith; family, personal, and career development,

I often hear pain and confusion. Because of overextension in ministry activities, serious relationship erosion in regard to spouse, children, and key staff is all too common.

Even when no apparent consequences of neglected or broken relationships are evident, the real emotional cost is usually greater than what is initially reported by pastors during LifeMapping. The gradual and cumulative effect alone of a pastor's education, sophistication, professionalism, and success can, over an extended period of time, erode the spiritual power that comes from genuine and continual submission to Christ. It is essential that spiritual leaders, and indeed all of us, have the awareness, courage, and humility to have safeguards of accountability in place.

Putting spiritual and emotional matters squarely on the table; seeking help early; being in authentic, interdependent, accountable, missional communities and teams helps church leaders avoid some of the many pitfalls they encounter. As Wayne Cordeiro says, "Whenever I see something going wrong in someone's life and ministry, I ask about that person's daily journaling in God's Word. Invariably there has been a breakdown there." Iron sharpens iron; relationships that are developed lovingly can support and encourage leaders in the battle.

One additional force at work in pastors can not, of course, be minimized—the real and present enemy—Satan. As the great deceiver, Satan's job is to find our weaknesses and to render us ineffective through specific, often subtle, attacks in those vulnerable areas. We can be sure, too, that his attacks will be minimal—until we choose to do something significant for God.

We believe that God has given all leaders—for their own good and for encouraging dependency upon Him—at least one Achilles' heel. It is imperative that church leaders—as well as all other Christians—personally identify and name each of their areas of weakness, and that such openness actively be part of any strategic preparation for significant ministry. God knows these weaknesses, our spouses know them, and the Enemy knows them. Each weakness represents a vulnerable target for Satan's selective darts. For one leader, it might be a tendency to wallow in self-pity when someone is critical of him. For another leader, it might be a tendency to avoid a decision or to escape unpleasant confrontations. For a third person, the trigger might be anger with dysfunctional responses such as sarcasm, put-downs, or uncaring behavior.

Not only must each weakness be identified, but an effective defense for each type of attack must also be in place. In my (Dan's) experience—working almost constantly as a pioneer/developer in frontline high-stakes assignments—my defense system has emerged gradually. My most effective strategies have been built around previous attacks. Each time some new attack occurs, I evaluate it prayerfully and ask myself, "What can I do next time to recognize this weakness as soon as it is targeted and to protect myself from harm?"

Pastors and other church leaders are no less vulnerable.

Questions to Consider

1. What might be the result if every leader in your community began developing a more precise and intentional strategy of spiritual development?
2. What kind of positive impact would such a strategy have on their personal effectiveness in ministry?
3. How much difference would this impact make on the congregations whom these pastors serve and on the congregations' abilities to influence their respective communities?
4. What measures can church boards and congregations take to support their leaders, remove the barriers, and provide the means and the space for their leaders to "go and grow" spiritually and authentically in community?

Case Study 1

Pastor's Spiritual Life:
Alan Nelson, Senior Pastor and Workshop Leader, Scottsdale
    Family Church
Scottsdale, Arizona

I (Dan) met Alan Nelson in 1987. He sat in one of my first sessions of revitalization clusters, a group of fifteen Wesleyan pastors in Irvine, California. I'll never forget this occasion because the night before all of my notes had disappeared from my computer as I prepared in a nearby hotel. I'd spent half the night in prayer, trying to recover my thoughts and asking God to help me know what I should cover. With some sense of peace and exhilaration I spent most of the first session unpacking the concept of the pastor's heart and brokenness, combining Psalm 138 with 2 Corinthians 12:9–10. Alan Nelson, a pastor in Mission Viejo, was exceptionally attentive. He was seated just to my right at the front table, and more than the others, he seemed to grasp the concept of releasing God's power through our weakness.

Afterward, Alan came forward and engaged me in conversation about the notion of brokenness. During subsequent months we discussed this concept repeatedly. This lead to Alan's doing a thorough biblical, historical, and contemporary research project. During this comprehensive study, Alan traced hundreds of examples of brokenness and eventually published them in a book titled *Embracing Brokenness: How God Refines Us Through Life's Disappointments.*[5]

Alan teaches the process of being spiritually broken as a part of God's character-building process. He shows how true servanthood is not built on skills or position, but on those very character traits God has built through brokenness.

In addition to being a prolific writer and well-known workshop leader, Alan has been the senior pastor of a rapidly growing church, which he and his team planted nine years ago in Scottsdale, Arizona. A few months ago, after twenty years as a pastor, Alan went full time into a ministry of writing and speaking about leadership development.

I don't know what else we talked about in that first under-prepared cluster session. But I do know the result of that serendipitous seed being planted within the receptive soil of Alan's heart. God has used it in the lives of hundreds of other pastors, multiplying the concept of brokenness and the ongoing condition of the pastor's heart.

4

Life-Giving System 2:
Corporate Intercession

The use of laser beams is common in today's world. Lasers are used for corrective eye surgery, removal of tattoos, carving images into wood, boring holes in metal, and a host of other creative applications.

A laser beam is, of course, simply light that is concentrated into a single, powerful stream. The concentrated power of the light allows the laser to do the work that light generally could never accomplish. The power of a laser is similar to the discovery made by young summer campers who experiment for the first time with a magnifying glass. With practice, these campers can take a piece of magnifying glass and concentrate the sun's rays on a piece of bark until smoke emerges. Then, by focusing the sun's energy, they burn their initials into the wood.

Similarly, when the prayers of God's people are focused, like a laser, on a single issue, dramatic results often occur. For example, I (Gary) remember an incident of corporate prayer in a church I pastored a number of years ago. A young man in his early twenties was diagnosed with cancer. The news shocked the church as well as the young man's wife and two small children. Immediately, however, the people in the church began to focus their prayers specifically on his healing. Through God's gracious power, the young man was healed and more than twenty-five years later continues living a healthy life.

The second life-giving system essential for generating spiritual energy is intentional and focused corporate intercession. Prayer has always been an essential component of the Christian's life, and much valuable training and teaching is available on developing personal prayer strategies. Effective prayer movements also mobilize and gather large numbers of people for specific prayer. Although corporate prayer is an essential part of all churches, only a small percentage of churches in this country have their own specific strategy for corporate prayer. When they put together their ministry plans, they pray *for* and *about* the plans, but prayer is not *in* or *part of* the plan.

Missing, then, is an *intentional strategy* with substantial emphasis placed on building spiritual energy through an intentional focus on corporate prayer. Although prayer has been emphasized in books and workshops for more than a decade, only rarely do we find churches able to point to a significant prayer strategy that has been verbalized and activated. This critical life-giving system, although always acknowledged as overwhelmingly important, is in all too many churches underpracticed and underorganized.

It is common for churches to appoint people or set up groups to take charge of missions, Christian education, music, and other areas of church life. Rarely, though, is an individual or team appointed whose primary task is to ensure that the prayer life of the church is becoming healthier, stronger, and more reproductive each year. Instead, prayer is usually seen as an auxiliary, behind-the-scenes activity, and not among the visible, articulated tasks and goals of the

> . . . prayer is usually seen as an auxiliary, behind-the-scenes activity, and not among the visible, articulated tasks and goals of the congregation. Churches give lip service to prayer's being essential, but too often prayer is not part of a church's strategy.

congregation. Churches give lip service to prayer's being essential, but too often prayer is not part of a church's strategy.

Prayer will always be part of church life and there will always be those who feel called to pray. But to be effective, *a prayer strategy must be intentional and focused.* Just as strategies and goals are articulated in other areas of church ministry, prayer should be approached the same way. To do so will not despiritualize it! Articulating a corporate prayer strategy involves the following two activities:

1. identifying intercessors and having a person, or persons, whose responsibility and focus is to nurture and reproduce intercession teams such that prayer will reach a more powerful level throughout the congregation each year;
2. choosing leaders who have a strong burden for prayer, understand the strategic role of prayer, and have the abilities to
   - reproduce and facilitate various intercession teams, each with its own specialty;
   - provide catalytic leadership for significantly increasing effective prayer, and to work alongside the pastoral staff in shaping creative and more powerful strategies each and every year.

Areas of Focus

Two of the essential areas on which intercession teams should focus are

1. the particular blockages to ministry and relationship that the church is experiencing; and
2. the untapped potential that exists in every church and must be brought to the surface.

Blockages can be removed by concentrating the power of prayer on the top "sticking points" of the church until each is removed. In one church, for example, the blockage might be the lack of an effective strategy for reaching unchurched persons. In every congregation are one or two key individuals who have the proper gifts and even the training to reach the unchurched but who have not been adequately challenged to get involved. Focused prayer is often the key to identifying the problem, finding the gifted individuals, releasing their potential, and reaching the unchurched. Before long, several effective bridges to the community may well become established. If we are faithful to ask God to answer our specific requests, untapped potential can be released by prayer.

Working Together

Another way to describe an effective corporate prayer strategy is to think of the relationship in football between a quarterback and a wide receiver. Sometimes this relationship becomes almost mystical. During the 1980s, when the San Francisco 49ers were dominating the National Football League, Joe Montana often leaned back and threw the football with all of his might. To many of us, he didn't seem to be even looking where he threw the ball. Seconds later, however, Montana would watch Jerry Rice extend his hands and see the ball drop, almost miraculously, right into them!

Churches with experienced intercessors continually recount similar occurrences. Their behind-the-scenes work results in a solution dropping into the lap of those who have struggled with a problem for weeks. As I (Dan) work alongside congregational teams, I frequently experience the exhilaration felt by Jerry Rice. God will miraculously provide a piece to a puzzle as teams of intercessors begin to pray. Invariably, I find that individuals, both internally and externally, were praying for the church and me. In my ministry I, in fact, always have one or more intercessors praying intensely and specifically for every ministry conversation in which I am involved. I believe that trained and committed intercessors are at least as essential to a ministry organization as administrative assistants, organists, or any other paid staff member.

Still, in every area of expertise and giftedness—with the exception of intercession—large congregations have a combination of volunteers and part-time or full-time staff. Churches are willing to compensate teachers, janitors, bookkeepers, and landscapers but not those who devote themselves passionately to seeking God's wisdom, direction, and intervention through prayer. This is beginning to change, with a few congregations adding a minister of intercession to the staff. Perhaps churches should consider compensating directors of prayer in the same way that they do Web-site designers, tax accountants, or those with other similar expertise. Intercessors, as much as any other ministers, are worthy of their hire (1 Tim. 5:18).

It should not be surprising, then, that one essential ingredient in an effective prayer strategy is that every leader be adequately covered by prayer support from experienced and properly gifted intercessors. The warfare described in 2 Corinthians 10 and Ephesians 6 is very real in churches today, especially among those who seek to break out of the status quo and their comfort zones. Whenever a congregation decides, for instance, to shift the corporate focus away from itself to reach the unchurched, spiritual warfare will occur. Add to this the current lack of volunteers and shrinking financial resources among all denominations, and the stage is set for a range of disruptive power encounters.

At stake in these spiritual battles are the hearts and minds of members. The results will be either, largely depending on the amount of corporate prayer, powerful victories or discouraging defeats. Indeed, training in and activating corporate prayer are essential components that will increasingly determine the viability of struggling congregations.

How does a congregation form and nurture an intercession team? The following ideas will help you get started.

Step One

Find one or two persons who have a burden for prayer and who are able to gather others with a similar burden.

Invariably, God has already placed in congregations, regardless of size or location, one or more persons with a burden for prayer. In most instances, congregational leaders have not realized who these passionate individuals are or what an incredible contribution they might make.

Intercessors do not have to be selected from the current pool of visible or outgoing leaders. Often, church leaders don't notice potential leaders of intercession teams simply because their talents remain hidden. No one notices them or invites them to pull together a prayer team. Sometimes, too, other leaders incorrectly conclude that, unless a person has been around a long time and is well known by the congregation, that person isn't qualified. Or it's feared that the person might make a mistake or drop a plate. At other times, faulty assumptions are made about a person's readiness for ministry, and that person's potential is underestimated because current leaders expect perfection.

Much of the fruitfulness in a congregation's future ministry depends, in fact, upon discernment in recognizing the subtle qualities of key individuals who might otherwise be overlooked. Most often, simply by asking, leaders can identify the intercessors in our churches. Certainly, it will take more time at the beginning to get a person operating effectively and in alignment with the rest of a congregation's ministry. But within several months, crossover will occur, and the chosen person will become a leader, selecting additional persons for the intercessory team. When this happens, acceleration and multiplication of ministry take place.

Step Two

Encourage the first person you identify to find a friend with a burden for prayer.

Part of the unique challenge of identifying intercessors is that they often do their work in private. Those who pray are instructed in Matthew 6:6 to enter their "closet," or inner room, shut the door, and pray to their Father in secret. When two or three persons, however, begin to share their burdens in prayer, the answers tend to be more apparent and more frequent.

Step Three

Develop a prayer strategy.

As soon as three to five people have covenanted to meet regularly for prayer, they are ready to begin developing a prayer strategy. Very simply, a prayer strategy contains several activities that are intended to raise the level of prayer throughout the congregation during the next twelve months. The intercession leader in most cases needs only to ask the team, "What can we do during the next year to take prayer to the next level?" One person responds and then the next. Before long, several ideas have been sparked, and the details for the strategy fall into place rather quickly. It is surprising what people can do when they are empowered.

Step Four

Begin forming specialty teams.

Start adding additional members who are burdened for particular ministries or particular kinds of prayer. Many churches, for example, are able to form a team that prays for the senior pastoral couple and their children. Another team might be focused on the other pastoral staff, or members of the leadership team, or perhaps one strategic ministry such as youth.

Other teams can be assigned to pray for each major area of emphasis, such as evangelism, equipping, or church planting. In one church my wife and I (Dan) visited, we noticed several people moving slowly along each row of chairs, stopping briefly at each chair. We found out later that they were praying for the person who would occupy that place during the worship service and that every service is covered in prayer by several specialty teams. These specialty teams had been created as an outgrowth of the prayer teams' strategic prayer and planning over the past several months.

Identifying Where Your Church Is in Intercession Team Development

These steps might not be as easy as they sound, but they are easy to identify. Do you have a leader? Has the leader been able to form a team? Has the team developed a strategy for the next twelve months? Has the team been able to internally reproduce teams according to specialties? Each of these steps is measurable. A church can determine at any point the status of the intercession-team development.

About five years ago, I (Dan) gave this assignment to one church in the Tidewater area of Virginia. Periodically, I checked back, and the pastor assured me that he was pleased with the steady progress among the intercession team. When I happened to visit his church at the three-year mark, I was truly amazed by how this church had been transformed by one faithful team of intercessors.

The pastor showed me a designated room where more than 130 intercessors gather each week. They close the door and pray to their heavenly Father. They have moved, tentatively and awkwardly, from an introductory level to an intermediate level, and eventually to an advanced level, where the impact of their prayer is obvious to most members. Prayer has become the single most powerful life-giving ministry in this church.

In another church, however, the results were quite different. I gave the same assignment and checked back several times over the next six months. The first person the pastor selected found another person, and they immediately began to disagree about when to pray or how to pray. Is it any surprise that this church remained stalled and stagnated? If a church has trouble forming this first team, it does not bode well for the future.

Finding Intercessors

Intercessors tend to be people who already spend a major portion of time in prayer. Their giftedness draws them naturally to spend time in prayer each day. To recruit intercessors, look for the following five traits:

1. *A person who prays.* Ask people in your church to whom they would turn if they needed prayer. Ask who in your church prays about an hour a day.
2. *A person who attracts others.* Does someone seem naturally to draw people together? Is anyone able to facilitate the development of a group?
3. *A person who respects the leaders of your church.* Intercession is a very personal type of ministry and involves a great deal of trust, transparency, and confidentiality.
4. *A person with expertise in building and maintaining relationships.* Intercession teams flourish on relationships. "People work" is often high-maintenance work, and the intercession team needs a leader who can minister to the team. This is not a lean and mean organization machine, which is a corporate view of ministry. Rather, it is a lean and keen organic movement—an organic movement of Spirit-empowered, radical, missionary peoples.
5. *A person of either gender.* Although the majority of intercessors are women, intercession is not an exclusively feminine journey. There is a danger that prayer can be relegated as a secondary source of power for the church. John Eldredge offers an excellent reminder that men can be both wild at heart and excessively intimate and tender in their relationships. Men who resonate with the mighty warriors of David can be deeply in prayer one moment and ready to raise the sword the next.

    Also, at the birth of the early church in the Upper Room were Peter, John, James, Andrew, Philip, Thomas, Bartholomew, Matthew, James the son of Alphaeus,

Simon the Zealot, and Judas the son of James. These men, all with one mind, were devoting themselves continually to prayer, with the women, including Mary the mother of Jesus, and with His brothers (Acts 1:12–14). There can be women's prayer teams, men's prayer teams, and teams with both men and women.

The important thing about prayer, as well as the people who perform intercessory prayer, is that it cannot be purely mechanical, programmed, or institutionalized.

When people pray, missionary movements are born. It is the beginning of revitalization, renewal, revival, or restoration.[1]

Questions to Consider

1. What might be the results if your church were able to double or triple the amount of effective prayer over a period of several years?
2. What kind of impact would this increased prayer have, especially if the prayers were focused on particular obstacles or unique opportunities?
3. How much of a difference would increased prayer and its impact make to the morale and momentum of your ministry?
4. What would it take to develop an intercession team in your church this year?

Case Study 2

Corporate Intercession:
Bobby Collins, Church of God (Cleveland, Tennessee affiliation)
Newport News, Virginia

Pastor Bobby Collins had tried everything. He'd been to every workshop and read every book made available to him. He wanted his church to grow, and he worked day and night toward that end. As a Church of God pastor in Virginia, he was part of a group of churches in the state known for being among the most progressive in its denomination (The Church of God, Cleveland, Tennessee). Each year they brought in different outside trainers to help their pastors stay current. I (Dan) was invited to work with Bobby and about ten other pastors during the mid-1990s. Toward the end of the first session I asked them to begin accelerating prayer in each of their congregations. I explained that the best way of doing this was to form an intercession team. First find a leader. Allow the leader to form the team. Allow the team to form a strategy. Then get out of the way.

Five years later Bobby attributed this one lesson to the steady surge of growth in his church. During my last visit, Pastor Collins had more than 100 intercessors who met regularly in a room reserved exclusively for their use. He had no idea exactly what they did. But he was thoroughly convinced that there was a high correlation between what the intercessors did in that room and the steady answers to prayer that occurred throughout the congregation. Those answered prayers had affected hundreds of transformed lives, and a doubling of the congregation's size during the next five years. Another five years have passed since that last visit to Newport News. Pastor Bobby's recent e-mail assured me that prayer continues to be the key factor in their exceptional growth. They've hired a prayer specialist, Russell Evenson, to take prayer to a higher level still. Pastor Russell also teaches other churches about prayer throughout the United States and overseas as well.

The Newport News congregation has doubled again, and they are now in five services. In order to better reflect their vision, the congregation have changed their name to WOW, for World Outreach Worship Center!

The WOW Center is saturated with prayer activities every day of the week. Everyone is invited Saturday evening, early Sunday morning, and Wednesday evening. Other intercession times are assigned throughout each week for groups of men, women, youth, and Hispanics.

5

Life-Giving System 3: Spiritual Disciplines

My (Dan's) life has been richly blessed and formed over the years through an abundance of caring mentors. None was more powerful than my own parents. In a small town in eastern Nebraska, they read the Scriptures with my two sisters and me each evening. At their prompting, we memorized by rote key texts and recited them around the table until they were deeply engrained in our memories. My parents created an environment in which God's Word permeated my soul and penetrated my heart. The Word became for me truly "powerful and sharper than a two-edged sword." I would not be in ministry today if not for that divinely inspired spiritual regimen.

Thanks to my dedicated parents, by the time I was ten years old I was able to recite more than one hundred key verses from the Old and New Testaments. During my adolescent and young adult years, those powerful, embedded truths, more than any other factor, kept me from straying permanently from my spiritual moorings. I've traveled in many countries and for three decades have been called into complex and inflamed situations involving churches as well as leadership teams. To provide me with the spiritual energy and resilience to keep doing this with faith, hope, and love, I cannot improve upon the simple priority of spiritual disciplines modeled by my parents in Nebraska.

The Importance of the Spiritual Disciplines

Recently, seminal works by several writers—such as Dallas Willard, Eugene Peterson, and Richard Foster—have challenged churches to reconsider their beliefs and practices in the spiritual disciplines. This stream of literature was an important wake-up call.[1] Much of the church had fallen asleep during the 1960s and 1970s and had developed an unhealthy dependence on one-hour worship services. Christians depended on the pastor's sermon to feed them spiritually for an entire week. What a contrast to the "self-feeding" first-century Christians who "studied the Scriptures daily" and eventually turned the world upside down.

Much of the failure of churches to be healthy and reproductive during the last quarter of the twentieth century is in direct correlation to pitifully low levels of discipleship training. Scripture teaches clearly that each one of us is responsible for our own spiritual development. So many aspects of our lives are either uncontrollable or only partially controllable. Spiritual development, however, is one area that is, with few exceptions, fully controllable for most Christians.

One of the primary hurdles we have to overcome is the comfortable Christian life being modeled by leaders in too many churches. We've settled for the wrong list of requirements for leadership. Many churches are now reaping the consequences of embracing leadership development courses borrowed from graduate business schools, and neglecting the basic disciplines practiced in the early church. Two additional obstacles that prevent us from focusing on our spiritual development are lack of discipline and the tendency to get busy with other priorities. The root word of disciple is *discipline.* Self-control is one aspect of the fruit of the Spirit. Often when Christians think of discipline and self-control, they conclude that their lives will become dull and boring. They fear that if they become intentional, organized, or regimented in their discipleship practices they'll end up with a lifeless list of do's and don'ts. Nothing could be farther from the truth. Discipleship can and should be the most exciting adventure in the world!

The purpose of Life-Giving System 3 is to address the huge spiritual void in the life of the average church member. In other words, it is not enough that pastors take responsibility for staying in shape spiritually (Life-Giving System 1) or that an intercession team has formed to take prayer to a higher level each year (Life-Giving System 2). For the body of Christ to have enough spiritual energy to reproduce, every Christian must be intentionally encouraged to take responsibility for his or her own spiritual development (Life-Giving System 3).

In the area of spiritual disciplines, throughout history the church has swung repeatedly from the extreme of excess to the extreme of omission. Today, we are seeing the emergence of an exciting new asceticism, one that is based on the lifestyle of Jesus and His disciples.

The old asceticism was characterized by legalism. It lacked the freshness of religious practices built on a sincere desire to know God more intimately and to experience his power so as to be more effective in service. The new asceticism draws on several action-oriented biblical metaphors: athletes who want to compete for the prize, soldiers who cannot afford to get entangled in the affairs of everyday life, fishermen who toil all night, and hardworking farmers whose livelihoods depend on understanding how to sow and how to reap (see 2 Tim. 2:1–6).

If an aspiring athlete desires to be an all-league champion, he or she knows doing so will require a regimen of strict training over a period of at least several years. Similarly, if church leaders are to develop spiritual champions in the church, it will take more than following a "one-minute management" approach to maturity.

My (Dan's) athletic experience consists primarily of water sports. In preparation for water polo games and swimming meets, my high school and college coaches designed a number of conditioning exercises aimed at developing both strength and stamina. One of the most effective methods was tying my feet to the edge of the pool with a couple of strands of surgical tubing. I then swam as far as possible away from the edge of the pool, stretching the tubing, and attempting to hold the position. Each day, I tried to increase the amount of time I held my position. This regimen of rigorous training was a significant factor in building a team that became California state champions and, since then, has allowed me to remain in shape as I continue to swim laps for exercise.

For people today who want to stay physically fit, training methodologies and opportunities abound. Perceptive trainers provide trainees with a customized combination of routines that will produce the best results without causing injury or too much displeasure. Often, this involves a cross-training approach, which includes prescribed distances or times in several different sports, such as biking, swimming, or jogging.

Just as physical conditioning produces endurance and strength for the body, spiritual conditioning is essential for a Christian's long-term health and vitality. If they so desire, both individuals and churches can raise the level of their spiritual conditioning. The authors mentioned earlier detail numerous spiritual disciplines, including solitude, Bible study, fasting, frugality, and service. Just as a trainer or athlete chooses regimens, so church leaders, team members, and those who are seeking to grow can harness a combination of spiritual disciplines that will enable God's power to be maximized in their lives. The net effect is that each person, by accessing the power of the Holy Spirit through the spiritual disciplines, can greatly increase his or her spiritual strength and stamina.

Victories in spiritual battles depend to a great extent on what has occurred *behind the scenes* of a church in individual and corporate spiritual conditioning routines. This invisible block of time creates spiritual preparation and character formation, and is referred to by Kevin Mannoia as the Iceberg Principle.[2] Most of the action is below the surface. What we see is only the tip of what is actually there; what is below the surface is responsible for what we see.

Several of the questions that I frequently now ask in my interviews with leadership teams relate to "the curtain." These questions help me to discern differences in the behaviors and attitudes of the leaders when they are "in front" of the curtain doing visible activities, in contrast to when they are "behind the curtain," acting as individuals or in a small group where they cannot be seen by the public. When I detect a significant difference in behavior between the two sides of the curtain, a corresponding lack of spiritual below-the-surface disciplines is usually present. The truth will eventually work its way to the surface. What we sow we eventually reap.

I recall one consultation with a large mainline congregation in the Midwest. A member of the congregation, who was a gifted corporate consultant, worked together with me conducting rigorous interviews with various people from the church. In our initial interview with the senior pastor he made it clear that he didn't want to discuss spiritual matters at all. When we presented our preliminary findings, one of the "core issues" we addressed was the spiritual life of the church. Because of the public nature of the meeting, however, we didn't address specifically the senior pastor's reticence to talk about his own spiritual life. It turned out to be a very significant core issue. This pastor's private life did not include any time for developing intimacy with God. Instead, the void in his life had been filled by a secret, adulterous relationship with a woman in the congregation. Eventually, the truth surfaced. From way behind the curtain, his behavior eroded the prayerful hard work of the leadership team and the congregation, and devastated the church.

Another aspect to address is the emotional needs of church leaders. Few people realize the amount of emotional energy that is drained from Christian leaders in frontline ministry. Bill Hybels, founding pastor of Willow Creek Community Church, used to believe that he could approach invincibility by simply keeping an eye on two gauges—the physical and the spiritual. He now gives equal attention to the emotional gauge, recognizing that his usefulness in ministry is similar to charging or discharging a car battery. A car battery can be drained fairly quickly by leaving the lights on. It takes much longer, however, to recharge it to full strength. Bill tells how he found himself dangerously emotionally drained and describes the intentional steps he took—and continues to take—to keep his emotional battery charged and his gauge at normal.

Let it be clear that when we refer to spiritual energy we are not describing some "New Age" philosophy. We are advocating, in fact, the very "old age" and original first-century discipleship. Christians are moving either forward or moving backward at any given moment. Like a battery, our souls are being either depleted or replenished. Participating in spiritual disciplines is the best way to prevent burnout and to keep our emotional and spiritual batteries fully charged. Also, it is a way to help fill the spiritual energy void in our congregations. If leaders are modeling a vital spiritual life (the pastor's heart allegiance), when corporate intercession is thriving, and when members are practicing rigorous spiritual disciplines, a church is well on its way to having spiritual energy and filling the "spiritual energy void."

> Like a battery, our souls are being either depleted or replenished. Participating in spiritual disciplines is the best way to prevent burnout and to keep our emotional and spiritual batteries fully charged.

What might happen in your congregation if most members were becoming more spiritually fit each year through ongoing practice in the spiritual disciplines? What kind of positive impact would that have on their personal effectiveness in ministry? How much of a difference would it make on the congregation as a whole and on its ability to influence the community?

In each of the life-giving systems it is important to establish a starting point, or baseline, by which to measure future progress. On a one-hundred-point scale, the baseline on generating spiritual energy through spiritual disciplines, compared with other life-giving systems, is probably as low in most churches as any of the life-giving systems. The surface of this untapped reservoir of power has only begun to be scratched. It stands to reason, then, that even a small increase in spiritual discipline activities will produce a dramatic surge in spiritual energy.

The impetus for increasing spiritual energy through the life-giving system of spiritual disciplines can come from many sources. First, a progression could be followed similar to that for increasing spiritual energy through corporate intercession:

1. Find a leader who has a burden for spiritual disciplines.
2. Form a spiritual disciplines team.
3. Develop a strategy for taking spiritual disciplines to a higher level during the next twelve months.
4. Reproduce specialty teams according to different functions within the ministry of spiritual disciplines.

Nothing is more compelling, however, than the modeling of leaders as well as the enthusiasm of those who are already practicing spiritual disciplines. These disciplines can be infused into every aspect of church life and encouraged and modeled by the pastor and leaders. Many churches have done creative things to get people on the same page. Some have met the Lord around Bible readings, others have provided retreats to get people going in spiritual disciplines, and yet others have worked the disciplines into their teams.

Of all of the life-giving systems, spiritual disciplines can be the most challenging to grasp and the one that most leadership teams have difficulty getting started. Doing so can, however, be surprisingly simple. Similar to starting an exercise program, the main thing is not to think about it for too long; "just do it."

Experiment as a Team

The best way to get the disciplines firing is to begin experimenting with various spiritual disciplines in your teams and small groups. Start by agreeing to begin practicing certain disciplines with your leadership team. Chances are that spiritual disciplines already appear in some form in your church's core values or vision statement. If not, perhaps this would be a good time to revisit both statements and see how spiritual disciplines could best be included. Do your statements, for example, refer to making disciples? What is your strategy for equipping leaders? Modeling the practice of spiritual disciplines and holding each other accountable for exercising them is an obvious natural fit into the categories of discipleship and leadership development.

A good place to begin modeling is by concentrating primarily on prayer, Bible study, and sharing your faith as the most important spiritual disciplines. We often assume that active church members and leaders are already making space for these practices, regularly if not daily. But in many cases that's not a valid assumption. As discipling continues, other spiritual disciplines periodically can be introduced into the regimen. One caveat, however, for those who start down this road: the temptation is to become fascinated with more exotic and unusual disciplines and move beyond these foundational disciplines. Not all spiritual disciplines are equally important or equally effective in building disciples.

This is an age in which various fads in leadership development come and go. It is of note, however, that the leadership teams that are most advanced today in terms of making disciples and equipping leaders all have some rigorous expectations in place for personal Bible study, prayer, and sharing one's faith.

One pace-setting church that has seen explosive growth, New Hope in O'ahu, Hawaii, has, from its inception, engaged in a spiritual discipline that shaped the "DNA" of the church. During the first year of planting that new church, Wayne Cordeiro and Dan Shima met daily to study the Scriptures. As the founding leaders, they made a commitment to each other to study the Scriptures regularly at a pace that enabled them to read the entire Bible in one year. They sought to see their current situation—a snapshot of the main things going on in their lives and ministry at the time—through a particular lens—that is, their encounters with God in their daily readings. They also held each other, and others who joined them, accountable for aligning their attitudes and behaviors with Scripture.

The value of this simple yet challenging assignment became quickly evident. God spoke to them each day. They each recorded in a journal the main message from the three to four chapters-a-day regimen, writing out a simple prayer asking God to help them apply the message of the day in their own lives. They shared that daily message with each other and began to share their "messages" with other people throughout the day. This very personal and relational approach ignited sparks in dozens of relationships and created an enormous amount of spiritual energy as the church grew. These sparks have been both transformational and transferable, and this spiritual discipline has become "the secret weapon" of that ministry.

I (Dan) had the opportunity to discover this "secret" of New Hope in sixteen days of observation, interviews, and participation over a three-year period. I don't usually devote this amount of time at my own expense to the study of one church, but I was attracted by the spiritual energy in this church, which was somehow being transferred from its leaders to its attendees.

On our first visit to New Hope, my wife and I interviewed several key leaders and some of the regular members. We also attended a "Doing Church as a Team" conference, and although some of the attendees were outsiders, the conference was held mostly for training New Hope people. During that time, we witnessed a massive Easter celebration, great music and preaching, and the exceptional leadership of Wayne Cordeiro. But that did not explain the incredible radiance of the people. What we witnessed could not be attributable just to the use of spiritual gifts, enthusiastic coaching, or exceptional leadership. We were convinced that there was much more to it.

The explanation came later when Wayne invited me to attend a practicum in Honolulu with twenty-four senior pastors, most from large churches on the West Coast. During this time, I actually experienced and learned how they build such radiant, reproductive disciples at New Hope. What, you might ask, is so unique and exceptional about New Hope? Of all of the factors contributing to the health and growth of New Hope, their use of life journaling—explained below—is the single most important one.

As part of the intense mentoring experience of this practicum, we observed several typical days in the life of Wayne Cordeiro. We got up each morning at 5:30 a.m. to jog with Wayne along the beaches of Honolulu.

Then we met to study the Scriptures. We read three to four chapters each day, some from the Old Testament, some from the New Testament, and a sprinkling of Psalms.

After reading these chapters for about thirty minutes with four or five of us at each table, each of us selected the verses that most spoke to us individually and wrote them verbatim in our life journals. Then we wrote a sentence or two, explaining as best we could what the verses meant and how they applied to our lives.

At the top of the page we wrote the message that had bubbled up as we interacted with the text. The last few minutes were spent writing out a prayer and asking God to help us live out that particular message for the day. We then recorded the text, the message, and the page number on the table of contents, after which we spent about ten minutes sharing what each of us had written.

Although this exercise is so elementary, none of these seasoned pastors expressed skepticism or manifested resistance. Most pastors and congregations would claim to have a Bible study of some kind in place, but "life journaling" is much more profound than it seems on the surface. The pastors were all connecting genuinely with the exercise, and they could see immediately how their leadership teams' participating in such an activity would have an enormous impact on them.

I could not have guessed that twenty-four senior pastors, with churches having an average attendance of from five hundred to five thousand, would have been so energized by such a basic exercise. After three days of following this simple pattern, I did not spot a single skeptic among the pastors. Virtually all of us, in fact, left the conference with a box of Life Journals to begin using with our leadership teams immediately upon our return.

I went home a changed person.

It certainly has made a huge difference in the life of New Hope. The Life Journal that started with a small team as a personal discipline is now a printed volume and is part of the resources available at New Hope. The journal itself is a daily-Bible format consisting of passages from the Old and New Testaments, creatively linked to give a balanced diet. (Those who follow the format daily for a year read the Old Testament once and the New Testament twice.) After reading, the participant records the Scriptures that stand out for him or her and writes *an observation, an application,* and *a prayer.* Finally, the participant answers the question, *"How will I be different today because of what I have just read?"* A place is also provided for prayer requests and a table of contents on which the participant writes the date of the entry, the title he or she has given each journal entry, and the key verses.

All over Honolulu on any given day, attendees of the ten thousand-member church, including Wayne Cordeiro, can be seen in coffee shops reading their Bibles and journaling. They share what they've learned with each other, both in teams and at home, and have something from God's Word to share as they meet people who need it along the way. Additionally, since members are reading the same section, Wayne's sermons have added impact when he refers to a text that was read during the previous week. So Bible study, prayer, and sharing one's faith are natural parts of the daily lives of the people involved in the ministry. No wonder that church has so much spiritual energy.

This simple discipline in the life of the church has become foundational, not only to its spiritual development and formation but also to its leadership requirements. Many read-through-the-Bible-in-a-year resources exist, but unique to the Life Journal is the way it's incorporated seamlessly into New Hope's advanced leadership development system. *This simple regimen has, in fact, emerged as the main requirement for leadership at New Hope.* By their frequent reference to Life Journaling and, even more so, by example, Wayne Cordeiro and the other leaders encourage young disciples to begin and sustain this basic spiritual discipline. It is a staple in team relationships.

Most of New Hope's teams incorporate a time of reading Scripture at least once a week, and they may also share the highlights of the texts from the previous week. Thus, the teams maintain a high level of encouragement, modeling, and accountability. Additionally, when leaders are asked to give a brief devotional, they are already prepared and can select an appropriate word from the table of contents in their Life Journals. Prospective leaders therefore become trained in sharing what they're learning with others in a natural and contagious manner.

As has been noted, the reading of Scripture in public has become a common practice among New Hope's leadership teams. This practice reinforces the boldness needed to be a postmodern Christian and forms a powerful collective witness throughout Honolulu.

Life journaling has had a powerful effect on the spiritual lives of my wife and me. We not only practice it ourselves but also enthusiastically pass it on wherever we go. We introduce it as the "secret weapon" for any revitalization strategy and team ministry in a church or group that has called us in for coaching. (This resource can be ordered in a variety of forms from www.enewhope.org.) I've tested life journaling during the past two years in more than fifty congregations. The results are more powerful than any other resource I've used in leadership teams. The experiences are so simple and pure. They remind me of my first year on a missional, frontline team in post-Christian Europe. There, our leader, Bud Hinkson, also had the foresight to ground us in the discipline of reading Scripture.

No resource is more powerful for healing and transformation than the daily study and application of God's Word. It is sad, though, that only a small percentage of today's leadership teams in congregations make this spiritual life-giving strategy a priority. Is there a correlation between the neglect of this one practice and the prevailing irrelevancy and impotency of our witness in the marketplace? In my mind, the jury is no longer out.

Questions to Consider

1. How active are your church leaders in spiritual disciplines?
2. What Bible reading plan are they using now?
3. Imagine the difference that might occur in your setting if all of your leaders were practicing life-journaling Bible study at the beginning of each day.
4. What would it take to begin implementing the plan outlined in this chapter?

Case Study 3

Spiritual Disciplines:
Gary Rodriguez, Steve Bentley, and Max Wilkins

Scores of pastors are now true believers in the spiritual discipline known as life journaling. Three that have particularly impressed me (Dan)—Gary Rodriguez, Steve Bentley, and Max Wilkins—have all been personally mentored by Wayne Cordeiro. Each has been radically transformed by making this discipline their top priority. Their marriages, their teams, and their closest friends have all been favorably impacted by their dedicated practice of this simple strategy. Life journaling helps leaders become self-feeders in God's Word. Through their local networks and various workshops, these three pastors have also been effective in reproducing life journaling in the lives of other pastors.

Gary Rodriguez is the lead pastor of Twin Oaks Church in San Jose, California. Gary was president of a broadcast company before entering ministry. He met Wayne Cordeiro five years ago through a mutual friend. Gary had been journaling by himself off and on for a year, then he attended a practicum at New Hope. As a result, he realized how critical it was to make life journaling a high-level commitment.

It wasn't long before the transformation of Gary's heart through regular journaling became evident to his leadership team. In order to find out more, some of his team went to a "Doing Church as a Team" conference at New Hope. Upon their return they formed their own team. Now they meet once a week for seventy-five minutes to share how God is working in each of their lives as they feed daily on the same passages of Scripture.

According to Gary, the unity and power they have gained through this interaction is unstoppable as its impact seeps deeper into the congregation. Life journaling is the primary tool for personal development of the leaders at Twin Oaks. Gary anticipates that most of the congregation's future growth will continue to be attributable to this "behind-the-curtain" commitment by the leadership team.

Steve Bentley ministers in Boise, Idaho. I met Steve several years ago during a practicum break at New Hope. Like the other twenty-four pastoral participants, Steve's lifestyle and ministry have been changed forever by the skill set that was passed on to him from Wayne. Steve's contagiousness about life journaling in particular also caught the attention of Bill Easum. Since then, Steve has facilitated two online seminars with Easum, Bandy, and Associates. As a result, scores of other pastors are now enthusiastically journaling with their leadership teams.

Max Wilkins is the senior pastor of the Family Church in Gainesville, Florida. Max acquired the practice of life journaling while on staff at New Hope. When he arrived at his new assignment in Florida eighteen months ago, life journaling became a core strategy.

Max preaches on journaling, and he offers a class six times a year, entitled "Developing a Heart for Devotions." Testimonies are featured regularly from those whose lives have been transformed by becoming self-feeders in God's Word. Every ninety days, Max persuades attendees to begin journaling through introducing a new daily Bible reading guide—conveniently posted on their Web site—for life journalers at Family Church. In other winsome ways, Max makes references to life journaling at least twice a month.

Through all of these patient, non-legalistic means, Max is creating a culture where life journaling is a shared value. The key is consistent "behind-the-curtain" disciplines by leaders, and members' regularly sharing stories of experiencing authentic life transformations. Max estimates that 15 to 20 percent of the thirteen hundred attendees regularly journal—and the percentage is rising.

6

Life-Giving System 4:
Mentoring Relationships

Carl, a gifted senior pastor in his forties, was being overwhelmed by attacks on his personal leadership style. Those who complained were not able to temper their criticisms by valuing his exceptional leadership assets. Although Carl tried to remain faithful to the work, the effect of a two-year attack eventually took its toll. Carl has found another assignment several states away, and an interim is pastoring his former congregation for the next eighteen months.

These kinds of attacks have conditioned many pastors to protect themselves. Thus, they don't risk the consequences of disclosing their weaknesses. A result is that many church members have had unrealistically high expectations of their leadership. Some congregations have, in fact, become known for chewing up and spitting out their pastors, always hoping that the next one will be perfect. Consequently, far too many congregations are not able to deal constructively with the critical needs of leadership development and with the sensitive task of enabling and empowering their leaders. It's time to challenge and overcome this prevailing dysfunctional view of leadership. Old, established patterns of denying and de-emphasizing weaknesses must give way to more biblical and effective approaches.

A countertrend, however, is emerging. Many people are looking for more authenticity and honesty in their leaders, and an increasing number of pastors are able to reveal their weaknesses accurately and unapologetically. This megashift is causing pastors to be more open to mentoring relationships, forming teams, and surrounding themselves with gifted people who have complementary strengths. These pastors can then rejoice in and support the giftedness and accomplishments of others in areas where they themselves are lacking.

This idea isn't new, but maybe it's been forgotten. In 2 Corinthians 12:9, Paul presents his case for coming to grips with weaknesses: "'My grace is sufficient for you, for power is perfected in weakness.' Most gladly, therefore, I will rather boast about my weaknesses, so that the power of Christ may dwell in me." A refreshing move has been away from leaders wanting to be "the man," the most gifted and the most indispensable one. Instead, with increased self-awareness and greater dependence on the power of God, pastors can position their congregations to grow by recognizing and encouraging the talents, gifts, and strengths in their congregations.

Something wonderful happens when pastors and leaders are able to realistically assess their strengths, weaknesses, and humanity. They not only become better leaders but also are able to recruit staff and lay leaders who have greater skills and abilities. These pastors can build leadership teams according to complementary strengths and find people who, because of their unique strengths, balance the overall effectiveness of the current team.

One of the most freeing moments in ministry occurs when leaders discover that they don't need to pattern themselves

> Something wonderful happens when pastors and leaders are able to realistically assess their strengths, weaknesses, and humanity. They not only become better leaders but also are able to recruit staff and lay leaders who have greater skills and abilities.

after anyone else, but that each leader is unique. We as consultants frequently encourage leaders to be more authentic, and to work on showing more of their unique, God-given personality. Leaders who try to pattern themselves after another person find that they either fail to live up to their model or become exhausted trying. The challenge is to allow God to release us as Christians to be the people He created for our own unique ministries and to encourage others to do the same. Ministry teams can then be formed on the criteria of overall fit and suitability, not on the availability of anyone who is willing to meet the need.

One indispensable skill set for leadership development is the ability to form and participate in mentoring relationships. Church leaders' doing so enables those around them to release others in exhilarating, reproductive ministries. Healthy and reproductive leadership teams know how to create an environment in which each individual can be fulfilled with joy, and finish well the life they were meant to live.

Leadership development cannot be sustained in local congregations without accountability and mentoring relationships. Mentoring research and strategy manuals have proliferated since 1990. With the impressive amount of new information available, a composite thesis may now be presented: Effectiveness in leadership is due largely to the quantity and quality of mentoring relationships.

Effectiveness in leadership is due largely to the quantity and quality of mentoring relationships.

No area has received greater attention in recent years than church leadership development. Yet, despite the record number of books and tapes being produced, too few pastoral and lay leaders are actually being produced. One of the most important areas that must be addressed in coaching leadership teams is the subject of how to develop, nurture, and preserve pastoral and lay leadership.

Levels of Mentoring

J. Robert "Bobby" Clinton describes four essential types of mentoring: upward, downward, internal, and external.[1] Of these types, *upward mentoring* is the most difficult type of relationship to find. *Upward mentors are those whom you perceive to be ahead of you in age, experience, size of congregation, or degree of personal effectiveness.*

Those who are perceived as having the most to contribute are invariably, of course, the leaders in shortest supply. To compensate for this situation, leaders seeking an upward mentor must learn the skill set for taking the initiative to seek and secure upward mentors. Most pastors, however, do not naturally come equipped with either the desire to initiate a relationship of this kind or the skills necessary to do it.

> Upward mentors are those whom you perceive to be ahead of you in age, experience, size of congregation, or degree of personal effectiveness.

Most pastors perceive making such a request as presumptuous. Some pastors justify their inaction with careful reasoning: "If I were to ask for such a commitment, it might seem to be an unreasonable demand. Pastor Smith is a busy person. I need to respect his privacy. Besides, the risk of rejection is too high for me to take the chance."

For men born before 1965, the prospect of approaching a potential mentor can be overwhelming. They often relate it to memories of approaching a female classmate as a potential date. Awkwardness and the possibility of rejection flood their minds. In light of the Great Commission, however, pastors cannot afford to be captured by such inward-focused and self-conscious responses.

The challenge is not as daunting, though, to the current generation because of the predominant tendency of young men to "hang out" regularly with other young men and young women.

Much of the awkwardness is minimized because now genuine relationships are developed in a much more natural environment than was experienced in the last two generations.

Nevertheless, most pastors require some simple coaching in initiating upward mentoring relationships: "Sure it might be somewhat stretching and uncomfortable to make a list of potential upward mentors and begin contacting them, but let me help you think it through." Usually, all that's required is for the seeking pastor to take some time and think about which individual would make the most ideal upward mentor. Then it is often helpful to think creatively through possible approaches by phone or e-mail and ways of overcoming geographical distance or the frequency of meetings. With so much at stake, pastors could ask themselves the strategic question: "What are the costs to my ministry of *not* making upward mentoring a priority?"

On the other end of the mentoring spectrum, according to Clinton, is *downward mentoring. Downward mentoring is investing time in developing those who perceive you, the pastor, as being ahead of them in age, experience, size of congregation, or degree of personal effectiveness.* But, for the best of leaders, this type of mentoring often produces the opposite challenge: "What can be done to develop new leaders from among those who gravitate toward me?" If no one desires to be around you, the pastor, then you are still at the prementor stage of your effectiveness. If, on the other hand, you are constantly besieged by requests for mentoring commitments, then you need an efficient process for selecting those with the highest aptitude and desire.

Because of the sheer number of demands upon their limited time, many pastors mentor downward in groups or teams rather than individually. Weekly meetings

> Downward mentors are those who invest time in developing those who perceive you, the pastor, as being ahead of them in age, experience, size of congregation, or degree of personal effectiveness.

with the staff team are quite common. Much less intuitive, though, is the notion that pouring one's life into a few people over the long haul generates more fruitfulness with much less risk of burnout. Even a quick overview of the ministry of Jesus, however, demonstrates that He trained the twelve disciples primarily as a group, and only rarely do we find Him conversing with individuals alone. The apostle Paul, too, advised Timothy to find a few faithful men and women who can, in turn, find a few other faithful men and women (2 Tim. 2:2).

Somehow, Paul's advice doesn't seem to fit the hectic schedules of today's typical senior pastors. Instead, downward mentors often allow survival instincts to determine their scheduling patterns. They eliminate personal appointments whenever they can justify doing so, and they try to gather all of their leaders into one meeting each month. It's taken a long time and an unfortunate amount of pain in the form of epidemic pastoral burnout to learn that Paul's advice is just as relevant today as it was in the first century. What produces the greatest fruit for the kingdom—pouring one's life into four or five leaders over a period of several years? Or pitching leadership principles through PowerPoint presentations in auditoriums? The first is a more time-consuming and high-maintenance activity, but in growing leaders there can be no shortcuts, and pastors must understand that growth and development are high-maintenance activities.

Another mentoring relationship or category is *lateral mentoring*. This is *forming peer relationships where the purpose is to mentor and hold each other accountable.* Such mentoring relationships can take place with friends or associates within the same denominational system or fellowship of churches who are mutually perceived as peers and who agree to form a lateral relationship. This relationship is also called *internal mentoring.* One of the most encouraging trends today is the realization that pastoral peer networks are the most cost-effective means to revitalize congregations. For more than two decades, I (Dan) have been privileged to facilitate at least one such peer network each year. Typically, I will commit to a minimum of five and no more than ten pastors for all-day meetings each month, for a total of at least nine days per year.

Internal mentors are those who invest time with friends or associates within the same denominational system or fellowship of churches who are mutually perceived as peers and who agree to form a lateral relationship.

In no other environment is a peer able to experience more safety, honesty, and encouragement and to receive such effective team-building skills. By working within a single denomination, and within a geographical area that does not exceed a two-hour drive, members are able to concentrate on particular issues with denominational peers, all of whom come from a similar theological tradition. Communication and effectiveness are greatly increased once pastors realize that lateral mentoring is not just another program and that there is great value in opening oneself to peers for counsel and support. Among the greatest lessons in this unique setting is the discovery that all of us have blind spots. Other common revelations are that we are not to function as competitors but as interdependent comrades in the greatest cause on earth.

Breakthrough occurs when pastors have the courage to share their own pain or confusion, and then experience genuine care and life-changing counsel from their peers. After the breakthrough occurs, no one asks how many more sessions he or she must attend or what subjects will be covered during the next several months. Instead, members realize that this is a biblical umbilical cord. They look forward to contributing nourishment to and receiving nourishment from peers in a transformational, missional community.

Another form of lateral mentoring is *external mentoring*, which is *investing time with friends or associates from a different denomination and often from different vocational specialties who agree to form a lateral relationship*. Many pastors feel the need to talk to another trusted friend who is not enmeshed in the culture or politics of the same denomination. They want someone who can function as a neutral sounding board. Pastors are often willing to travel to another part of the country just to be with friends who can understand them, provide another perspective, and offer honest feedback.

External mentors are friends or associates from a different denomination and often from different vocational specialties who agree to form a lateral relationship.

Another encouraging trend that fosters this kind of cross-pollinating, "iron-sharpening-iron" environment is the city-reaching movement. In virtually every region of North America pastors are gathering for prayer and to relate authentically to one another. No longer are pastors able to justify and defend their isolation from one another. The unity described in John 17 is gradually becoming a priority. Instead of being perceived by an increasingly skeptical public as irrelevant, pastors are covenanting with and banding together for mutual support and discussions of how to become a transforming regional force. Jack Dennison and other pioneers have invested heavily in facilitating this national movement.[2] Scores of pastors in Houston, Texas, have covenanted, under the credible leadership of Jim Herrington. Pooling their resources, minimizing redundancy, and overcoming the impossible odds against collaborating in a Christ-honoring, sacrificial strategy, they lay down their lives for the greater cause of unity and community transformation. Many pastors have confessed their sin of unhealthful obsessions about their individual careers or the growth of their own congregations.

To maximize personal growth, it is desirable that every leader try to regularly interact in relationships from all four categories. The dangers of becoming overly committed can be minimized by efficiently managing a personal mentoring system.

Mentoring Skills

One essential skill must be mastered before a personal mentoring system can produce significant results. This skill is the way an individual enters and exits mentoring relationships. Most people, regardless of professional standing, have too few relationships, most relationships last too long, and most results are not nearly as satisfactory as they could be.

We humans tend to settle for whatever relationships come our way. We do not find it easy either to begin a new relationship or to terminate one that is no longer serving a useful purpose. Some relationships—such as those with God, our spouses, and our immediate family members—are, of course, meant to be permanent. And although a few other relationships are lifetime relationships, most others cannot be maintained indefinitely and may be occasional or short term. Most mentoring relationships that last beyond two years reach a point of diminishing returns.

To improve the quality of mentoring relationships, mentors must be more focused and intentional in arranging for and following through on them. Determine first how many relationships are needed in each category. Second, make a list of prospective persons with whom to mentor. Third, decide how best to approach each of those people. Once a mentoring relationship is agreed upon, ask several questions: How often should we meet? Where should we meet? What basic areas of our pastoring lives should we include? When should we evaluate our progress?

For almost two years, Bobby Clinton and I (Dan) agreed to a lateral mentoring relationship. The basic ingredient was a three-hour meeting every couple of months. Our focus was on challenging each other's strategic concepts. Except for a few minutes for personal updating and prayer, the entire exchange was devoted to exchanging information and perceptions on the most important strategies that each of us was beginning to develop. As a result, we left each meeting motivated to improve in the areas for which we had been challenged. Both of us had an assortment of other relationships, so we were able to concentrate on highly specialized and technical areas that were critical to our providing resources to other ministry leaders. Although Bobby and I would greet each other warmly if we were to meet, we have had very little personal contact since the lateral relationship ended.

Releasing the Gifts of God's People

Pastors and leaders should not only seek ways to be mentored, to mentor, and to form peer mentor relationships but also encourage mentoring relationships in their congregations. These often can be carried out best in team settings. Everywhere I (Dan) go, I say that we as Christians need to "grow as we go." Many times, a false dichotomy is presented between ministry and growing for ministry. Many churches have well-honed growth-and-discipleship programs to equip and grow people before they go on to do ministry. Ministers can, however, be discipled and equipped while they are on the job, which is the best mentoring relationship in which ministers can find themselves. Mobilization according to gifts can be done through both mentoring relationships and team relationships.

A folk story tells about three horses that were having a conversation in a wagon. The first horse said, "We're not moving!" The second horse replied, "Yes, that's true. I wonder why?" The third horse, who was obviously the most insightful, asked, "Do you suppose it's because there are no other horses out in front pulling?"

There is a direct correlation between the number of horses that are sitting in the wagon going for a ride and the number of horses out in front pulling (and leading the way). Indeed, one of the most stubborn and elusive challenges in ministry today is how to get lay people out of the wagon and involved in frontline ministry. The challenge is increasingly difficult in a time when almost all family members work and have multiple distractions and demands on their time. Because of fatigue or preoccupation with their own needs, people seem to prefer to consume, rather than to become involved in, ministry. Spectatorship, like a gravitational force, retards vibrant institutional and personal growth and limits ministry effectiveness. For their own true happiness, as well as for the missional cause to which all Christians are called, people must be helped to find their way out of the wagon and onto the team that is pulling the wagon.

One of the most proven approaches to overcoming the prevailing inertia in congregations is to help identify and release the gifts of team members. Of all the life-giving systems, none creates more satisfaction than a mentoring process. It is, in fact, needed to produce consistent, balanced, and healthy growth in people. Not only is a mentoring process easily transferable across ministries, it identifies giftedness and then challenges people to place themselves accordingly within the body of Christ.

All effective "mobilization" strategies have in common a preference for persons motivated by servanthood and suitability rather than by a sense of duty or duress. The Bible refers to spiritual gifts in Romans 12, 1 Corinthians 12, and 1 Peter 4. Ephesians 4 also speaks of people as gifts to the church, but such gifted people may also have a corresponding spiritual gift that empowers their leadership. The scriptural notion of giftedness is the proper centerpiece for all releasing strategies. Related human resources information—such as personality and temperament—complements the basic principles of giftedness and underscores the concept of suitability. In many situations, though, the "faithful few" have shouldered most of the work of the church rather than looking for and encouraging the giftedness of the many.

The Bible addresses the universal question of how to know God's will. Every human being has a vacuum that can be filled only by Christ. One's fulfillment in Christ cannot be ultimately experienced until one finds the place of service for which one has been divinely created. This core personal conviction can be an indispensable motivational ingredient for mobilization. Laypersons are highly motivated to discover where they fit in the body of Christ.

In one church, for example, a woman had worked diligently for the church in many areas. Because she was willing and did good work, she was asked to take on responsibilities in women's ministries, the choir, and Sunday school. When she learned in a spiritual gifts class, however, that her main giftedness was in administration, she focused her resources and energies in that direction. Instead of being worn out doing many things, she was energized and excited in understanding and accepting God's unique gifting for her, and she was released for fruitful and satisfying ministry. It is imperative for both churches and individuals that a gifts-based strategy build upon this divinely implanted motivation. If that woman had been mentored in a team situation or by a person who was sensitive to people's gifting, she would not have had to wait until a spiritual gifts class came along to find true joy in serving.

Similarly, all approaches to improving the life-giving systems should ensure that the focus is to facilitate *ministry* rather than administration. Too often, leaders see people in terms of tasks that help the leader rather than as individuals to be empowered for ministry through helping them identify and use their spiritual gifts. The goal is to release people to serve, not to plug them into various program slots. The vital difference between the two approaches will greatly affect the results.

Most churches today agree on the theological and practical importance of spiritual gifts. Churches don't have a problem acknowledging the existence of spiritual gifts, but have difficulty implementing a workable system to employ gifted people. This is particularly wasteful of God's resources in light of the growing shortage of volunteer workers and the necessity to limit volunteer service to one or two "hats" per person. Many churches are suffering from burning out a few dedicated volunteers, all of whom feel pressure to wear "multiple hats."

Since the average layperson has only two to three hours per week to invest in ministry, churches must offer them the one area of service that motivates them the most. When tasks have been assigned according to gifts, burnout is virtually eliminated. When individuals are using their gifts, they are happier, work more effectively, and are more willing and able to put in long hours without complaint. In the best of examples, where churches have concentrated on excelling in gift-based strategies, team members are asked to work less and to enjoy their families more because they have reproduced so many other teams of persons who enjoy using their gifts in their particular areas. These teams operate on the "grow-and-you-go" principle, and ministry and spiritual growth proceed simultaneously. Also, because people are encouraged, supported, and released, more teams are available in an area than are needed to work weekly. Four or five worship teams, for example, might emerge, enabling them to lead worship on a rotation basis and with the extra time look for other ways to provide worship opportunities both inside and outside the church.

Many churches encounter problems in finding people to serve because they recruit from a program-based approach rather than a person-based approach. A program-based church tries to employ people based on the church's needs. This type of church looks first to its own internal ministry needs and then attempts to find people to fill those particular needs. This approach places the emphasis on the program rather than on the person being recruited. The opposite approach is to look first to the person being recruited to discover that person's gifts, talents, and desires. Once a church has identified a prospective volunteer's motivations, it then connects the person with a role or ministry that matches his or her ministry personality. This approach focuses the church's ministry on the gifting of members and allows quick inclusion of new Christians and even seekers.

Mobilization and mentoring strategies have gone through nothing less than a revolution in recent years. Significant advances have been discovered by several leading-edge congregations that have adopted a missional teams framework for ministry. Congregations such as Mosaic in Los Angeles and New

Hope in Honolulu have discovered breakthroughs that are now replacing the last generation of gifts-based strategies.

Fresh Approaches

For the past two decades, most congregations committed to a gifts-based ministry used a sequential approach that was borrowed or adapted from Willow Creek or Saddleback. In short, congregational trainers would attend a workshop on gifts-based ministry and then initiate strategies soon after their return. The basic sequence was to "teach 'em, test 'em, counsel 'em, apprentice 'em, and monitor 'em."

Thousands of Christians are now experiencing the joy of serving others with their gifts as a result of these excellent gifts-based strategies. In the best of circumstances, however, these strategies to maintain quality control were elaborate, cumbersome, and time consuming. On the periphery, many congregations never got beyond the teaching stage, which amounted to preaching a series of sermons on gifts and then periodically offering training classes on a Saturday morning.

The major shift in the new generation of gifts-based strategies is to take a more relational, holistic approach. All of the previous steps have now been incorporated seamlessly into both small groups and frontline ministry teams. Teaching, testing, and counseling are offered on a supplementary basis rather than as a prerequisite for service. Everyone is encouraged to be in a group or a team as soon as possible, with few if any prerequisites.

No longer necessary is a centralized data pool or a centralized procedure for monitoring individual progress. As part of the relational discipleship approach, members of groups and teams recognize the value of gifts as they participate in various weekly activities. They constantly see the joy in volunteers and the effectiveness of gifts in operation all around them.

Members in these missional team environments often do not hear much about gifts until the subject comes up in a Bible study or in a group conversation. Instead, the primary emphasis is upon learning to serve others because that is what Christians do. The hallmark of a disciple is that he or she is willing to lay down his or her life in service for others.

Consequently, everyone is encouraged to get involved in an entry-level team of some kind, regardless of any knowledge they may have about giftedness. If, in fact, a member is not willing to serve outside his or her gifts, it is likely to be viewed as a sign of spiritual pride rather than an advanced stage of maturity in which one serves in only one's area of giftedness. "Finding faithful men and women" is defined in this context as allowing unproven individuals the opportunity to experience the joy of serving alongside others. Being faithful means being willing to do whatever is needed to spectacularly accomplish the mission without whining. Mature Christians remain humble servants, always willing to assist promptly when the occasion arises. Gifts are identified and confirmed primarily by the manifestation of joy and by exceptional results when a person serves in a particular area of ministry.

In missional team environments, the primary emphasis is placed on team members' inviting friends or acquaintances to join a group or to serve on an entry-level ministry team. In one instance, this might be asking someone to help a group hold a home Bible study that is suitable for people with little or no background in the Christian faith. In another instance, the invitation might just as likely be to join a team of men who will be washing cars on Saturday morning. After serving on several teams over a period of a year or two, some team members will emerge as leaders, gravitating to their area of burden with little need for guidance or testing. They will know it by the sensations they experience whenever they are serving in some specialized ministry. What they call the gift is not as important as the confirmation that something special is going on when they operate in a certain kind of ministry. They are now in their "zone."

Because only a small percentage of churches are actually operating at this advanced level, it is usually necessary in most churches to slow down the instruction of team members so they can understand how the components of gift-based ministry work simultaneously. These components—teaching, testing, counseling, apprenticing, monitoring—are useful when a supplemental track, rather than a prerequisite track, of gifts-based resourcing is deemed necessary. The following is a more linear and sequential approach to mobilizing and mentoring individuals to discover and use their gifts.

Teaching

This is the easiest and most exciting component for most churches. Since teaching is already an established function in most churches, introducing teaching on spiritual gifts is relatively easy. Many churches have taught about spiritual gifts from the pulpit, in Sunday school, and in special seminars. Churches who use the teaching method need to be careful, however, that they don't limit their spiritual-gifts strategy to just teaching. Too often a church can become inoculated against spiritual gifts because the emphasis is only imparting information, and a "we-tried-this-and-it-didn't-work" syndrome can result.

Testing

Several tools, or instruments, are available for matching people who have discovered their gifts with the current need for ministry service in the church. Testing instruments reveal information about the giftedness, personality, and temperament of each individual being mobilized. Instruments are available for each theological tradition, and individuals either take home an assessment or complete it as part of the teaching sessions on giftedness.

Counseling

When an assessment is completed, individual interviews are set up. Results of the testing are typically discussed in the context of a forty- to sixty-minute initial session. An interview form is completed and becomes the primary tool in helping the individual to find the place of service that is just right for him or her. This step should not be rushed. Sometimes it will require two or three appointments over a period of several weeks before the individual is able to decide which available position is best.

Spouses and family members are often involved in this important personal decision. Prayer over a period of time frequently leads to an adequate sense of peace and a clear sense of direction toward a particular calling. A ministry description is then written out and customized to that individual's unique situation. The job description contains clear responsibilities, expectations, and time frames. If something doesn't work out, volunteers know to whom they can turn to make an adjustment.

Apprenticing and Mentoring

Once a decision is made, the individual is assigned to a team with an identified trainer or mentor. The trainer should be the best-qualified person in that particular area of ministry. The newly assigned individual begins by observing the mentor in the actual ministry position. This stage is followed by the new person's attempting the same series of tasks under the observation of his or her mentor.

After two or three real ministry experiences, the new person is usually able to serve with minimal supervision. The process of "shadowing" is now complete. If something were to happen to the designated trainer or team leader, such as a call to another place of ministry, the shadow would be able to assume the position with little if any loss of momentum. Every new person, when he or she has served in a ministry for a few years, should be encouraged to become a trainer of other new persons. Thus, leadership can be multiplied rapidly as the described cycle is perpetuated.

Monitoring

Some churches maintain elaborate centralized monitoring systems, but these systems are quickly yielding to grassroots systems built upon trust within discipleship teams. Accountability for the spiritual lives of team members and for their responsibilities on the team occurs unobtrusively in the weekly rhythms of the team's study, prayer, and preparation for service. Encouragement and celebration are more apparent than correction. Dropped plates are recovered routinely on the assumption that we all want to improve.

When personal correction is required, the team member is taken aside in a friendly and courteous manner by the team leader. Feedback received in an environment of high-expectation mission is rarely taken personally. When relationships do break down, a more senior member of the ministry area is called upon to intervene. The person who is having difficulty is usually reassigned or given some time off to work on personal or family issues that are more important than their team activities.

In evaluating the extent of mobilization, it is important to have realistic expectations. One hundred percent mobilization of church membership is never a realistic goal, because at any given point in time a significant percentage of the congregation need care rather than being able to care for others. A realistic first-year goal might be to increase the level of congregational mobilization by 10 to 20 percent. Gradually, with continued development and reproduction of missional teams, it is possible to have 50 to 60 percent of the congregation involved in some kind of ministry team.

Another strategic resource for mentoring relationships and releasing gifts is LifeMapping.[3] Tom Paterson's association of life planners pioneered the concept of discerning the spiritual DNA within each individual. Rather than being restricted to the classical gifts or leadership styles, the aim is to find the identity of each individual's "snowflake" (wonderfully and uniquely made).

A two-day process with a professionally trained facilitator

provides the concentrated setting to review the chapters of a person's life to discern his or her top three talents. On the second day, the facilitator and the individual then determine how best to fulfill this individual's destiny by keying off of his or her unique identity. Paterson's process has been further developed and popularized in Rick Warren's book *The Purpose Driven Life*.[4]

In my (Dan's) own consultations with individuals in the process of leadership development, I refer to the lifemapping process as intentionally finding and staying in one's destiny zone. Wayne Cordeiro says that the purpose in leadership development is to find the "flag" deep within each person and then to let that person "fly it" on a team as soon as possible.

The mentoring process—be it upward, lateral, or downward—assists, simplifies, and accelerates enormously the process of leadership development.[5] Whether mentoring and mobilization are implemented simultaneously or in a more sequential and linear way, they go hand in hand in developing leaders who can meet the challenges of today's seismic shifts.

Questions to Consider

1. What might be the result if your church could double or triple the amount of effective mentoring over a period of several years?
2. What kind of impact would this have on the quantity and quality of leadership development?
3. What might be the result if your church doubled or tripled the percentage of people who have been mobilized according to servanthood and suitability rather than duty or duress?
4. What kind of impact would this have in reducing burnout and increasing ministry effectiveness? On the morale and momentum of your ministry?

Case Study 4

Mentoring Relationships:
Ray Ellis, Free Methodist Senior Pastor and Consultant Trainer
Willow Vale Community Church, San Jose, California

Ray Ellis attended the Diagnosis with Impact (DWI) training at Fuller Theological Seminary in 1982. At the time, Ray was the Director of Evangelism and Church Growth for the Free Methodist Church, based in Indianapolis. Carl George and I (Dan) were the primary trainers for this intensive eight-unit DWI doctor of ministry course. Sam Metcalf (now president of Church Resource Ministries), Bob Logan (founder of CoachNet and promoter of Natural Church Development), Bill Sullivan of the Nazarenes, and Steve Babby of the Wesleyans were in attendance. Most of the first-generation denominational leaders in the Church Growth movement of the 1980s were, in fact, mentored and credentialed through this high-end, quality-controlled approach to disseminating church growth expertise.

The first phase involved forty hours of classroom training, followed up by the attendees' performing three case studies during the next two years. The first phase required the attendees to assist in a field visit, and Sam Metcalf assisted me with a full-blown assessment of The Evangelical Free Church at Fullerton, while Chuck Swindoll was the pastor. Bob Logan accompanied me to a small church in Wrightwood, California. Ray Ellis went with Carl George on one assignment and later on several different assignments with me. Then each participant had to complete two additional cases on their own, but under the supervision of Carl George or myself. Ray was one of the survivors of this "Navy SEAL style" training who met with us on campus for forty additional hours of debriefing, advanced training, and certification.

Like many mentoring programs of this kind, DWI was closed down by the Fuller Institute within five years because it was too expensive to maintain. Our board decided that it was more financially viable to do workshops than invest in relationships with emerging denominational leaders like Ray, Sam, Bob, Bill, Steve, and scores of others. I believe in retrospect that decision was a huge strategic error.

Of all the life-giving systems, mentoring is the farthest from producing a quick return or a quick fix. At least a decade is, in fact, required to see a return on investment. During the last two decades, scores of leaders have caught a thirst for coaching and consulting congregations as a result of the mentoring experiences that were birthed during those seminal years at Fuller.

Ray Ellis and I remain close friends and colleagues today. Ray is finishing his fine career as a senior pastor in San Jose, California. He also serves as the National Director of Consultant Training for the Free Methodist Church of North America, and as a Mentor for Fuller Seminary, Menlo Park Campus, mentoring students currently enrolled in the World Mission class. The mentoring torch of congregational coaching was passed from John Wimber to me when he hired me at Fuller Institute before he was called abruptly to birth the Vineyard. I in turn passed it to Ray Ellis and others. Ray has since passed it on to a whole new generation of Free Methodist coaches. John Wesley would be proud of Ray.

Last year my wife and I were seated at a table with Ray Ellis and Gary McIntosh in New Orleans at our annual gathering of the American Society for Church Growth. At the same table were Gary Reinicke, Tim Matheny, and several others, all of whom had received their "field training" rites of initiation into the Church Growth movement primarily through a powerful field-based mentoring experience. They received their love of serving churches in the crucible of real cases amid the pain of real leadership teams, rather than in textbooks or classrooms. Each of them in turn has gone on in his or her respective calling to mentor scores of other agents of change, mostly pastors within individual congregations.

While sitting at that table, it became very clear that mentoring works!

7

Life-Giving System 5: Team Ministry

Cartoons have a way of crystallizing key issues. One of my (Gary's) favorite cartoons pictures a senior pastor sitting behind an extraordinarily huge desk. Across the desk from the senior pastor sit three assistant pastors in chairs that place them much lower than the desk. With a smile on his face, the senior pastor announces to his staff, "I want you to know that I believe in team ministry."

One of the hottest buzzwords during the past decade in both the corporate world and church community is *teams*. Read any business journal, and you'll see it. Take a trip to any bookstore, and you'll have no difficulty finding the best book on this subject. We hear this ubiquitous and somewhat confusing term used repeatedly in conversations with other church facilitators and among staff and lay leaders in congregations of all sizes.

Most senior pastors, staff, and congregations have the word *team* in their vocabulary, but when they "talk team" they don't all mean the same thing. Most congregations operate at a very elementary level, thus, when advanced teams discuss team concepts, they use terms that are foreign to the average congregation. What exactly is team ministry? How may a congregation embrace and implement teams?

What Is a Team Approach?

Most churches think of *team* as *people doing ministry activities together.* In most churches, ministry done in groups fits this definition—worship teams, prayer groups, outreach teams, and various other types of committees and task groups. Frequently, however, these groups are teams in name only.

Being a team in the way this chapter advances it involves more than accomplishing tasks together. For decades, groups in churches have accomplished tasks together. Establishing effective ministry teams, though, involves much more than creating a new program or changing the names of existing committees. Although traditional committees involve "people doing ministry together," those committees often have been formed by another committee or person, and they lack the key essentials of healthy, effective team ministry. This chapter is not, therefore, talking about renaming committees, boards, and task forces, giving them a more modern name. Team ministry occurs when people doing ministry together develop a vision and carry out plans they've had a part in conceptualizing. The team then becomes a ministering and caring community.

> Team ministry occurs when people doing ministry together develop a vision and carry out plans they've had a part in conceptualizing.

A "worship team," for example, although it might be doing many group activities, might lack the above essential characteristic of a team. One worship team recently asked for evaluation. This team is led by a professional music director who makes all of the decisions—from the choice of music to who will solo and what instruments will be used in each section of worship. Team members are told what to do, and suggestions are not encouraged. Expressions of opinion and disagreement are, in fact, seen as divisive and nonsupportive. Compliance often seems to be more important than positive results. Although this group of musicians may be called a team, they are too director-focused.

Consider an alternative situation in which a senior pastor of a large church is a member of his church's worship team. All of the team members have designated roles. The group starts its work for the coming Sunday during the week with everyone contributing to the design of the service. All members of the worship team are encouraged to voice creative ideas for future worship services. The leader works from the belief that the Holy Spirit is active and alive in each member of the worship team. Therefore, worship services are enhanced as each member of the team contributes ideas to the overall worship design.

Many churches still operate in a staff-designed and staff-directed mode. Laypersons are expected to carry out activities that have already been determined by a professional specialist. These professionally designed and centrally initiated programs are, it's true, easier to install and control than team ministries created and implemented by active and talented laypersons. The results, however, are usually less effective because members have not been sufficiently involved in developing their own unique strategies.

Characteristics of Team Ministry

Team-oriented churches are experiencing positive outcomes from their shift to a new team model. Following are some of the characteristics:

- *The vision is grass roots initiated and owned.* Ministry activities are carried out for the most part by the same team members who experienced the original inspiration for the strategy. Collective wisdom is at work. One person comes up with an original idea. The next person builds upon it. One plus one then equals more than two. Deuteronomy 32:30 teaches this principle with the question, "How could one chase a thousand, and two put ten thousand to flight?" The answer is that multiplication occurs exponentially through the unlimited spiritual power that can be released through bands of warriors, or teams focused on a God-directed and

Spirit-empowered mission. This principle is repeated in Leviticus 26:8: "Five of you will chase a hundred, and a hundred of you will chase ten thousand."

- *Staff roles (both professional and lay) are different.* The concept of leadership is reshaped. Rather than being the sole initiators and designers, professional staff members serve more as coaches and facilitators of vision. Although they don't abandon their vision-casting and leadership skills, they see that their job is to form strong teams, draw out the vision and talents of lay staff, and facilitate the process of strategy design. Team leaders see doing so as part of the team members' discipleship process. Most professional staff, though, have not been trained in this process, which is one reason team ministry fails to take root in many congregations.

- *Team members are connected to a compelling, owned vision.* This vision guides them in both familiar and unfamiliar situations, captivates their hearts and minds, and provides a criterion for decisions. Because the vision and mission are owned, team leaders and members are invested in carrying on even in difficult situations. Like the North Star, the vision enables team leaders to navigate with confidence when waters get rough, and guides team members back on course even when the team seems lost or unsure of its direction.

- *The teams are fluid and focused on a task.* Teams are extremely flexible. They focus on a particular task and then may disband or take on an entirely different project once the current project is completed. Because what they are doing is connected to a clearly articulated overall goal and focus, the tasks are valid only as long as they are needed to accomplish that goal. This, of course, is the exact opposite of what committees do. Committees are commissioned and tend to have a life of their own, often perpetuating their existence, even after the job is done. For teams, on the other hand, territory and position become unimportant. People hold their jobs lightly, in the sense of being an indispensable part of the task and team, and do not "own" positions or protect territories.

- *Team members acquire a deep-seated belief in the power and synergy of teams.* This quality is particularly important in the early stage of strategy development when everything seems to be in a perennial state of chaos. Members are called to a mission in which everyone has a part, and they believe they can solve whatever they are able to confront because they stand shoulder to shoulder and have developed a culture of dependence on both each other and the Lord. This attitude is not one of arrogance but of team confidence that together they can tackle any project.

- *Team members experience a climate of trust.* Team members are encouraged to express openly ideas, opinions, discouragement, and disagreements. Questions are welcomed. All members are able to say whatever they want, within reason, without people becoming upset.

- *Team members practice open and honest communication.* They endeavor to understand each other's points of view. Information does not flow from senior pastor to associate to team leader but rather in all directions (up, down, and sideways). Some of the best information and ideas may be shared in the parking lot, come from the prayer team, or be discovered through the grapevine.

- *Conflict is viewed as a normal means of exploring new ideas creatively.* Team members know how to process conflict in a healthful manner and constructively resolve strong differences of opinion. Disagreement is not viewed as disruptive but as constructive. Members believe, in fact, that constructive conflict produces creativity.

Making the Shift to Teams

Churches, however, too often take an unfortunate approach in changing to team ministry. They view it like an afternoon jog: it's something else to add to the existing list of things to do, and the hope is that something will "take" and lead the church to revitalized ministry. A sure route to failure is attempting change without first building focus, commitment, and spiritual grounding.

Preparing God's people for team ministry involves more than teaching, volunteer management, gifts assessment, or some program on "equipping." Megashifting to team ministry takes time, and it means developing a new way of looking at how to mobilize lay ministry.

In practice, the move to team ministry plays out in different ways. Some churches move to team ministry rapidly with a churchwide overhaul. Others add team ministry gradually on top of their existing structures. Others do not initially disturb the existing structures but choose to begin new teams alongside or in addition to what's already going on. Others do a combination of changes with a few teams inside and other teams outside the existing structures. The strength—and the frustration—of team ministry is that it cannot be defined as a single approach or program. Rather, it is defined as a mindset. It involves a change at the heart of individuals, a change in culture, core values, perspective, and practice.

> Team ministry . . . cannot be defined as a single approach or program. Rather, it is defined as a mindset. It involves a change at the heart of individuals, a change in culture, core values, perspective, and practice.

During the last several years, I (Dan) have coached more than one hundred congregations in megashifting to missional team ministry. These congregations have been in all regions of the country; from all denominational families; across the spiritual health spectrum from very sick to very healthy; in multicultural, urban, suburban, and rural settings; in sizes ranging from thirty-five to thirty-five hundred. The most important discovery that came out of this field research was the superiority of team ministry. Teams proved to be effective regardless of the particular context, church typology, or core issues involved. Church health and revitalization occur with greater ease, less cost, and greater acceleration where leaders megashift to team ministry.

Nevertheless, before taking the plunge into team ministry, it's worth noting that the journey is usually not as blissful as the experience reported by the "exceptional" teams often depicted in popular books and articles. Many churches, in fact, like other organizations, have tried teams and seen them stumble out of the gate. An effective church, however, will view the growing pains realistically.

In the first year of moving to team ministry, members are often uncertain as to how much voice they'll be given, especially in congregations in which the pastoral staff have been expected to be directive. Pastors are often tempted to take back control soon after incidents occur in which members drop plates. Some staff will conclude, incorrectly, that it's easier just to do the job themselves rather than rely on an unproved, uncertain, uncontrollable process. In the initial year of shifting to ministry-team activities, a certain awkwardness and tentativeness is likely. It takes time to come up with good ideas that can be implemented effectively by people who don't know each other and who've never ministered together. With little discretionary time available to volunteers, it's easy for them, and leadership, to become discouraged. Frustration may also occur when few tangible results are seen right away.

By the second year, though, crossover will have eventually occurred as the results of an empowered team exceed what could happen by a staff-directed, staff-designed program assisted by volunteers. Each year, the skill levels for team building and strategy development rise as lessons are learned and new leaders emerge. The aim is to move each team steadily from introductory skill levels to intermediate and, eventually, to advanced.

Teams in Scripture and in Church History

The current interest in using teams in the church is not merely a fad borrowed from business; it's based on principles and practices dating to the early church. Although corporate work teams, athletic squads, and military platoons offer positive examples of effective teams, team-based ministry is clearly best learned from studying missionary bands in Scripture. Indeed, beginning with the Cyprus and Cyrene team described in Acts 11 and led by Barnabas and Paul, missionary bands have been laying down their lives for others in frontline ministry teams for two thousand years.

Many Christians are unaware of the effectiveness of this original missionary wave and subsequent missionary waves throughout history. Paul's missionary band serves as an excellent biblical metaphor for twenty-first-century ministry because America has changed from a monocultural society to a multicultural society. Thousands of new tribes or peoples are spiritually hungry and are looking for spiritual connection. Today's unchurched, though, are finding answers just about any place other than the church, which is often seen as an irrelevant farce—confused, dysfunctional, divided, and bogged down in introspection and institutionalism.

A missional team framework reflects Paul's missionary band, building on the ancient foundations of the church. Such a framework, then, is not only rooted in the beginnings of Christianity but provides both message and metaphor for the future church. As such, missional teams provide a solution for practicing practical missiology and cross-cultural team ministry found in the New Testament, and for the missionary means of implementing the Great Commission.

Ralph Winter has brought to the atten-

> As we look at Paul's missionary band, we see the first example of practical missiology and cross-cultural team ministry in the New Testament and the missionary means of implementing the Great Commission.

tion of the missionary world that God's redemptive purpose has included two complementary structures that Winter calls "sodalities" and "modalities." Sodalities are groups that gather and qualify around some unifying factor—a common cause, interest, age, gender, or disciplinary standards—and where people have to meet standards to be part of them. Modalities are groups that have open membership, in which anyone who wishes to associate does.[1]

Winter uses these terms to describe the difference in the way Christians have moved out to accomplish the Great Commission and to be the body of Christ. In New Testament times, the two structures took the form of the missionary band (sodality) and the church (modality). During the Medieval Period they appeared again as the monastery (sodality) and the church diocese (modality). Today, they are seen in the form of parachurch organizations (sodality) and denominational structures (modality). Over the centuries, Christian sodality structures tended to be the groups that moved out more intentionally and together into the community, taking the gospel to where people were or performing specialized tasks for which they were uniquely gifted. Today, a missiological thrust is to encourage churches and denominations to provide a climate in which more sodalic structures, such as missional teams, can thrive. Churches that best respond to doing church as a team are often those that, although a modality, tend to have more of the missional characteristics and perspectives of the sodality, or parachurch, movements. These churches as well have a greater willingness to move into unchurched areas and to engage their community.

Whole new skill sets are needed by the next generation of church leaders. In a rapidly changing world, in which cultural shifts are taking place seamlessly, enormous confusion and ignorance operate about both church and mission. Current training and programs, however, are designed for a setting that has much more certainty and predictability. In a less predictable and less certain world, churches need to be cross-cultural rather than monocultural and more missional than institutional.

Paul and Barnabas model the correct skill sets in Scripture. In order to reach the Gentiles, their approach relied upon practical missiology and relational teamwork.

- Barnabas and Paul both had cross-cultural experience and were able to form an indigenous ministry. They provide the first manual in practical missiology, forming a particular team to reach persons in a particular context.
- They complemented and completed each other as key persons within a team-sized entourage. Each recognized what the other brought and valued the other person. They modeled giftedness, trust, healthy relationships, and Christian community.
- They were led by and in tune with the Holy Spirit, believing in God's sufficiency no matter what the circumstances.
- Barnabas was willing to allow Paul to lead the team, modeling how leadership succession is supposed to work in the church.
- Barnabas went on to mentor others on teams, notably Mark. Paul, because of his own giftedness, did not perceive Mark the same way. Barnabas saw what Paul could not see, and served as a strategic link and mentor. To reproduce, every team needs these strategic links and mentors.
- Paul covered a great deal of territory. He and his team did not stay so long in one place as to become institutionalized.
- Paul learned from Barnabas to empower people early in ministry and he continued this practice. They planted churches that became autonomous quickly and continued to reproduce other Christian communities.
- They developed new leaders by taking team members into real ministry settings, expecting them to rise to the challenge. Leaders were developed in the midst of challenging circumstances. Not all of the young disciples survived, but the best leaders emerged.

- They were able to secure authority from Jerusalem when it was necessary by presenting their church planting approach in ways that were perceived as favorable and appropriate. They modeled how sodalities can be highly autonomous yet work in effective partnership with modalities for a greater purpose.
- They developed an overall effective strategy, drawing upon Barnabas's history and credibility. When Barnabas's discerning gifts were creatively blended to Paul's catalytic gifts, an explosive, cross-cultural movement was launched.

Paul's missionary band was formed as a cross-cultural team; the story is as much about Barnabas as Paul. Together, they interacted with the more institutional, established church in a creative and healthy manner. Because their team was both mobile and frontline, it avoided the inevitable tendency to lapse into institutionalism.

The skills and patterns of these original missionary bands can be observed in the various waves of missionary bands through history. The practical characteristics of Paul's missionary team have been present in all of the great historical movements of Christian revival and growth, from Paul to present-day evangelistic and missionary strategies. Additional strategic clues for reaching postmodern peoples can be discovered in the unfolding interplay of sodalities and modalities following the first century.

Now is the time to reinforce the ecclesiological foundations of our church, to introduce practical missiology and learn from our biblical and historical origins, and once again become a catalytic force. Only by understanding practical missiology—that is, how the church contextualizes ministry, forms effective cross-cultural teams, and releases them to address issues in a particular context—can we effectively reach twenty-first-century people for whom the church is nonexistent.

Celtic Christianity

> Now is the time to reinforce the ecclesiological foundations of our church, to introduce practical missiology and learn from our biblical and historical origins, and once again become a catalytic force.

Perhaps the most impressive example of missionary bands or teams is seen in Celtic Christianity from the fifth to the eighth centuries. Here we observe repeatedly the same kind of misunderstandings that Paul and Barnabas faced at the Council of Jerusalem. Kenneth Latourette, for example, cites the irritation by the local bishops in Ireland and throughout the Alpine valley when they encountered one of Patrick's missionary bands, referred to as the Irish peregrine. Their faith and lifestyle simply did not fit into the bishops' diocesan pattern.[2]

George Hunter, in his seminal *The Celtic Way of Evangelism,* explains how Patrick's centers of learning were unique in that their monks migrated to distant countries. They formed missionary groups both to reach pagan populations and to elevate the morals of the nominal Christian populations near whom they settled. The apostolic teams sent out by Patrick, beginning in the fifth century, closely resembled Paul's missionary band in how they engaged barbarians in both conversation and in ministry.

The Celtic achievements as a movement were astonishing. As Hunter's study substantiates, Patrick's bands multiplied mission-sending monastic communities, which continued to send teams into settlements to multiply churches so that within two or three generations all of Ireland had become substantially Christian. Celtic monastic communities became the strategic "mission stations" from which apostolic bands reached the "barbarians" of Scotland, much of England, and much of Western Europe.

The ultimate cause of their disappearance in the two centuries following the Synod of Whitby in 664 was the control of the Roman way over the Celtic way. The Romans were more conservative, insisting upon cultural uniformity rather than allowing for shifts in methodology. Celtic Christianity adapted to the people's culture. The Romans wanted Roman cultural forms imposed upon all churches and people. In distinguishing between a church's tendency to be institutional or missional, hierarchical or team based, dictatorial or discipling, good code words are *Roman* or *Celtic* approaches to ministry.

The move toward team ministry is nothing more than a strategy for implementing the simple plan for church leaders in Ephesians 4:12: "To prepare God's people for works of service, so that the body of Christ may be built up" (NIV). The Reformers attempted to return to this New Testament pattern by advocating the ministry of the saints, but they soon reverted to a variation of the hierarchical professional structures they so adamantly opposed.[3]

Some may perceive team ministry as similar to project teams in the private sector. Stephen Schey and Walt Kallestad offer a reminder, however, that the foundation for team ministry is based on the core beliefs of church leaders, not the values of the marketplace. Christian convictions about humility and brokenness come from God, not popular psychology. The study of God's Word and prayer, not management-theory books, create the passion for team ministry and prompt team members' desires to yield to His will. God, not a corporate manager, is the instigator and sustainer of healthy and functional team relationships.[4]

Another key difference between missional teams and other kinds of teams is that the relationships on the missional team are more important than the tasks that have been assigned. Missional teams function as a hybrid between the best of congregational small groups and the best of task-oriented work groups. In such leading-edge congregations as Mosaic in Los Angeles and New Hope in O'ahu, a symbiotic, positive relation is increasingly found between the level of caring for one another and the team's level of performance. Evaluation for progress in team building at New Hope and Mosaic is as dependent on how members laugh with, enjoy, and care for one another as on the precision and excellence in carrying out their assignments. The two go hand in hand; you can't have one without the other. As personal prayer and Bible study are incorporated into the weekly regimens of missional teams, the excitement of carrying out the team mission rises, as does the level of excellence in each specific task.

Whatever It Takes

Are you ready to begin (or continue) the shift toward empowered teams? Experiences across the spectrum of church sizes and denominations are confirming that doing so is valid, essential, and worth the investment—whatever the cost or level of struggle involved. Remember, however, that once the transition has begun and your church has stepped onto the bridge to team-based ministry, there's no stopping or turning back. Whatever it takes to get to the other side, do it. The alternative is stagnation, frustration, and a ministry that operates significantly below its God-given potential. Seek God's will, then do it in God's power and grace.

Questions to Consider

1. What might be the result for your church if committees and/or commissions were changed to missional teams?
2. What challenges would be faced in converting to missional teams? What major fears and barriers would need to be overcome?
3. What positive results would be gained by overcoming those challenges, fears, and barriers?
4. How could you get started on the road to developing missional teams?

Case Study 5

Team Ministry:
Ron Kincaid, Sunset Presbyterian Church,
Portland, Oregon

I (Dan) first received a call from Ron Kincaid in May 2002. Ron
is the senior pastor of Sunset Presbyterian Church (SPC), a large
suburban congregation on the west side of Portland, Oregon.
He'd heard that I might be able to help SPC make the shift to
team ministry. I agreed to meet with their entire leadership team
for two full days of interviews.

But I sensed early in our initial telephone conversation that
making the shift wouldn't be easy. Two obvious reasons were
their size (2,500 weekend attendance in five services), and their
Presbyterian polity. The PCUSA Book of Church Order is
thicker than any other denomination's. Also, Presbyterians are
well known for seeking to do things "decently and in order." It
would be a challenge to help SPC—a large, established mainline church, with an embedded, historic, and theologically based
structure—in making the shift to creating and reproducing
ministry teams.

The good news is that everyone I met welcomed me as a friend.
All of the groups they had assembled were eager to learn about
thinking and operating in an entirely different way from a traditional Presbyterian church. The bad news is that I couldn't hand
them a program or diagram explaining systemically how the
process works in practice. This lack of instant transfer was frustrating for them—and for me.

Like many large regional mainline congregations, SPC was
filled with many engineers from high-tech industries who were
used to seeing plans with clear schematics. When I'd use phrases
like "this is something you must first experience to comprehend,"
or "this authority is more relational than hierarchical" the eyes
of many would glaze over. Much of their training, too, in human
resources management slowed down the communication

process. CEOs and the apostle Barnabas view teams through radically different lenses.

I told them that it would take about two to three years before this new way would become second nature. Those two years have passed, and I'm happy to report that Ron and his team have crossed the bridge. They are, in fact, more convinced than ever that teams are both biblical and effective in producing a reproductive church.

If the journey can be successful at SPC, it should bring hope to any congregation in America. The high level of difficulty experienced at Sunset Presbyterian has demonstrated that any church can make the shift to missional teams if it is willing to commit to the necessary steps involved in such a radical shift—and Sunset was. Credit goes to Sunset Presbyterian's leadership, commitment, creative thinking, and desire to be reproductive. Two years after they began, they have a thriving ministry team in place.

8

Life-Giving System 6:
People-Flow Strategy

Half of the ten life-giving strategies that contribute to revitalizing congregations have now been described. In the preceding five chapters, key strategies were introduced for increasing spiritual energy and developing effective leaders. Before describing the next five strategies for increasing people flow and charting amid change, it will be helpful to step back and look at the big picture. How were these particular categories determined? And what has been learned along the way that establishes confidence in these strategies as being critical in revitalization?

Mostly a Lack of Flow

We often are asked to meet with leadership teams to help them conduct a comprehensive diagnosis. Over the past three decades, we've consulted with nearly one thousand different churches. During my (Dan's) first ten years as a senior consultant at Fuller Institute, I conducted more than two hundred such visits. In most cases, my visit was preceded by the completion of a 125-question congregational survey. The intent in each case was to collect the thoughts and feelings of a cross-section of at least 20 percent of the congregation. Typically, these consultations required two full days on-site. Two consultants visited a church because two sets of eyes and ears are clearly better than one.

In an effort to uncover all barriers to a church's growth, the consultants intentionally examined the "body" from as many angles as possible. They walked around the facilities and drove around the community. They interviewed focus groups from the leadership and the congregation. They spent at least two hours with the senior pastor and his spouse to determine their hearts, their sense of direction, and their pain. The hard data (statistics) were balanced with the soft data (the thoughts and feelings of the people.)

Those visits often seemed like assignments of the famous television detective Columbo. Attempting to discern God's vision and direction, we were praying and asking questions to find the truth and explore the realistic possibilities in each particular situation. Finding the truth in congregations is, unfortunately, usually quite elusive. We must often circle around several times until we discover the "jugular." Then, several weeks later, we returned with a ninety-minute report to the leaders in which we summarized the strengths, weaknesses, bottom-line potential, and recommendations for future growth. Our goal was to discern a path for the leaders that would help them maximize their growth potential. In most situations, we followed the oral report with a fifty-page report that arrived within four to six weeks. Both of us wrote several drafts before sending a final report to the staff and lay leaders, who then took a minimum of several weeks to digest our findings.

The Old Way: Fifty-Page Reports

Recently, I (Dan) had to face one of the greatest challenges of my life—clearing out my house in preparation for a major move from California. My wife and I are both pack rats. Rather than sort through our belongings each month, we prefer to put items in a box. We always intend, of course, to sort through the box later and to keep only the essential items. When we misplace an item, rather than take the time to make a thorough search, we just purchase another one en route to an appointment. Because of our passion for ministry, we assign a low priority to tasks such as sorting.

With this particular set of deeply shared values, the boxes naturally tend to grow fairly rapidly. When we accumulate several boxes in a room, rather than take the time to sort through them, we invariably carry them to the garage. As soon as I get a day free, I *intend*, of course, to sort through them. You've probably guessed that because of calls for help that come with active ministry the sorting never happens.

Can you imagine how embarrassing it is for me, who helps others identify and address issues in their lives and ministries, to dig into a mountain of boxes in my own garage? The accumulation in hundreds of boxes after twelve years in one place was overwhelming. Thanks to a dedicated team who believe in my ministry and who were given special mercy, my wife and I have now tamed the monster, and the garage is clear.

One of the most interesting discoveries during that full month of sorting was the two large boxes of diagnostic reports on local churches. In one corner of my garage, I stumbled upon scores of reports completed during my decade at Fuller.

The New Way: The Napkin Interview

The sobering truth is that we can now deliver almost the same value using a much shorter and less expensive process. In as little as five to ten minutes, in fact, with either a pastor or a few members of a congregation's leadership team, we can come to remarkably similar conclusions as those contained in a fifty-page report. Sometimes, though, I (Dan) will spend as long as ninety minutes with a group of leaders before I reach a conclusion. The issues that members identify can be lumped invariably into one of four baskets, each representing a critical congregational void: generating spiritual energy, developing effective leaders, increasing people flow, and charting amid change. It's not important to know why these same voids are always present, but every single congregation with which we've worked needs at least some work in each basket.

This five-minute "napkin analysis" proves to be almost as accurate as the two-day, two-consultant comprehensive analysis and 125-question survey. Does it not make sense, then, for us, as good stewards, to devote the bulk of our resources to filling those voids with life-giving remedies rather than spending most of our time and money assessing the patterns and trends?

Following are questions related to the four voids that are asked during an initial five- to ten-minute napkin survey with congregational leaders:

1. *Generating spiritual energy.* If I could show you a way to double or triple over the next twelve months the overall spiritual energy in your congregation through prayer and basic discipleship, would that be helpful?

2. *Developing effective leaders.* If I could show you how to double or triple over the next two years the number of leaders who are growing spiritually, experiencing vibrant and authentic relationships, and using their gifts passionately on ministry teams, would you be interested?

3. *Increasing people flow.* If I could show you a way to accelerate to several years rather than several decades the flow of people with no or low church background who become responsible and reproductive team leaders, would that make a difference in your church?

4. *Charting amid change.* If I could show you how, during these turbulent times in society, to map a future that increases the two-way flow of communication between church leaders and grassroots attendees and enables you to streamline your structure so that twice as much ministry is occurring with no additional cost, would you be interested?

What Can Be Done About the Obvious Lack of Flow?

It's unfortunate that most congregations never get beyond diagnosis. From what we know now, diagnosis is a comparatively easy first step. Although the questions and instruments may vary, the conclusions drawn from most surveys or from studies completed by congregational coaches (regardless of costs) are not all that debatable. In most instances, the result of these assessments point irrefutably to an inadequate flow of people. And the potential solutions all relate somehow to increasing spiritual energy, developing leadership, and learning how to navigate the future amid unprecedented societal shifts. To address the deep systemic issues related to each of these critical voids, life-giving systems for each void are best addressed simultaneously. By far the most practical and cost-effective means of releasing people-flow strategies is to form and reproduce missional teams.

Considerably more difficult than diagnosis is knowing how to change these stubborn patterns of inadequate people flow. The desperate need of this hour for congregations of all sizes and shapes is for someone to come alongside leadership teams and show them how to become an authentic missional community and how to reproduce the fundamentals of ministry in others. Behavior modification is usually not fun, is often not easy, and seldom occurs without third-party assistance. If leadership teams can be shown how to focus their limited energy on the four critical voids, their odds of developing a healthy and reproductive ministry that accelerates the enlisting and equipping of contagious disciples (people flow) greatly increases.

Chapters 3–5 introduced several life-giving systems for generating spiritual energy. Each system is triggered by a series of questions such as "How is the pastor's heart? Does the church have a prayer team and how effective is it? How many self-feeders in God's Word do you have?" The leadership development void (Critical point B) is the one most frequently perceived by leadership teams. If we were to ask any group of pastors what is their greatest current need, they'd invariably say, "Identifying and developing leaders." Chapters 6 and 7 of this book introduced ways to fill this profound leadership void with two high-impact strategies—mentored relationships and team ministry.

Understanding and *increasing people flow* is the third critical void found in virtually every congregation. It is a concept that is much less understood and rarely identified as a need. People flow is the means by which unchurched people move toward responsible involvement in local churches, and it includes the process of conversion, restoration, and maturation. Without probing this crucial arena, without activating some new strategies over the following twelve months, there is little hope for realizing and sustaining significant change. The pervasive and deep-seated patterns of stagnancy will remain. Without profound understanding of and extensive experimentation with people-flow strategies over a period of several years, there's little chance of favorably affecting extremely low reproduction in the average congregation.

> People flow is the means by which un-churched people move toward responsible involvement in local churches, and it includes the processes of conversion, restoration, and maturation.

Congregational executive boards have, unfortunately, a much clearer idea of their cash-flow patterns than of their people-flow patterns. Pastors and lay leaders may be experts in pinpointing money flow—financial leaks, fiscal problems, and monetary growth—but they are woefully naive about how people flow *into, through,* and *out of* their churches. Yet, in terms of a church's ultimate missional purpose, which of these stewardship flows is more important?

Becoming conscious of and facilitating how people are drawn into a church and given the opportunity to hear the gospel is an essential and critical focus. People flow into the church by two major pathways: "front-door" and "side-door" pathways.[1]

In a front-door pathway, people arrive on the church premises

Figure 8.1

because of the programming. It may be the music, preaching, or attractive facilities that draw people like a magnet through the front door. In a side-door pathway, people come to the church less directly. They "slip in the side door" because they have been met and ministered to in the community. These side-door ministries can be as varied as the more visible front-door ministries.[2]

Churches that use the first approach concentrate on a gospel by attraction; those that use the second approach focus on a gospel by sending, that is, sending people out to live and present the gospel as salt and light in the community. Theologian Johannes Blauw refers to these contrasting forces as *centripetal* and *centrifugal*. *Centripetal* action draws people toward the center of a church's activities. This was characteristic of mission activities in the Old Testament. *Centrifugal* action, however, moves people away from the center of activities to an outside strategy similar to the approaches in the New Testament. Both are means by which lost and broken people can be led to wholeness and salvation.

At least one missional team must understand the people-flow

strategy in your church. Are people coming in through the front door or the side door? Is this flow accidental or intentional? How many of these people are flowing out the back door without any impact being made on their lives? By developing people-flow strategies, your church can provide the framework for setting goals, for strategy preparation, and for measuring missional effectiveness. Through focusing on people flow, your church can help unchurched people to believe and belong, and Christians can be helped to reach full spiritual maturity. In addition, through monitoring your church's people-flow strategy, church leaders will have a better understanding of the reasons people attend as well as exit your church.

One of the most important things to understand about people-flow strategies is that all activities of the church are interconnected. The pastor's class, education, outreach, and small groups work together and should relate to one another consciously and intentionally. Leaders must become much more sensitized to the flow—or lack of flow—of people from one activity to the next.

One way to look at people flow is by using New Testament fishing imagery. Jesus taught His disciples to become "fishers of men." As fishers of men, pastors and lay leaders must know where the dominant fishing spots are located and how to bait the hook of the gospel for each spot. Regardless of whether leaders are aware of it, a process for "catching and cleaning" new believers can be identified in all healthy and growing congregations. Although some awareness of people flow exists in every church, the actual process by which it occurs is usually less intentional than it could be—often hit or miss.

Two essential and interrelated life-giving systems contribute to people flow. The first is designing and monitoring an appropriate people-flow strategy. Practical steps and guidelines for creating and expanding people flow in your congregation will be described during the rest of this chapter. The related life-giving system—identifying and training people for lifestyle evangelism—will be the focus in chapter 9.

Developing a People-Flow Strategy

In the early years of outreach, churches often try many different approaches. Sooner or later, they discover that certain approaches work better than others. Remember, however, that no strategy lasts forever. In today's turbulent world, it is, in fact, a safe assumption that whatever used to work for churches will probably be replaced by something else.

As in the other life-giving strategies, the people-flow strategy cannot be left to take care of itself. It is essential that a team of persons be responsible for identifying not only the major pathways but also the major blockages to forward movement. Congregational executive boards have a much clearer idea of their cash-flow pattern than of their people-flow patterns. A people-flow team is as crucial as is an accountant or business director to the cash flow of a church. The people-flow team is responsible for providing information that will enable the leadership team to create an overall strategy for enlisting and equipping new disciples. The people-flow strategy enables a church to "cast their nets" on another side of the boat and remain more sensitive and faithful to Christ's commands to be fishers of men, women, boys, and girls.

> Congregational executive boards have a much clearer idea of their cash-flow patterns than of their people-flow patterns.

Several new measures are helping congregations to plan programs that more effectively relate to growth pathways. Congregations are learning to conserve and channel their limited energy into ministries of low costs and high fulfillment. They've also learned that, in the United States, the term *people* refers not only to families, lineage, and social class, it also includes tribes, castes, and clans.

In some cases where people-flow analyses have been conducted, approaches to preaching, calling, and education have changed. If studies show, for instance, that a basic problem for people is loneliness, ministries then can reformulate programming to center more on themes of peace, forgiveness, love, and opportunities for informal fellowship.

People-flow analysts are sensitive to people in change. Such analysts believe that many of the current strategies, though well intentioned, are ineffective because they work against the current of social movements. Upward mobility, for example, is a reality of current society. When viewed as a neutral force, it can work for or against church growth. Churches that recognize the values of the upwardly mobile (avid self-improvers) can—without compromising convictions—provide the appropriate recognition of people who are caught in its current. Such adjustments illustrate the difference between upstream (against the flow) and downstream (with the flow) strategies.

People-flow analysts also recognize and anticipate social currents, believing that in developing missional strategies, it is better initially to move with the current rather than against it. In the example of upward mobility, discipleship strategies can focus increasingly on imparting an important essence of Christianity, which is not about meeting our own needs but about laying down our lives in sacrificial service for others. Recognizing upward mobility is not the same as approving its effects. Similarly, downstream strategies should not be interpreted as being exclusive or elitist.

Denominational strategies should attempt to reach as many classes and distinct ethnic groups as resources permit. During the past two decades, mainline denominations have been planting churches among newly arriving Asians and Hispanics. As the social and economic conditions of these newly arrived immigrants change during the next generation, a new wave of churches will be required to assimilate the new arrivals, who will, in turn, begin their "upward" journey. Some people have criticized these demographic groups as being intrusive on "the American way of life" when, in reality, they provide an opportunity for effective ministry. The simple truth is that the church can reach and nurture more people if it is not insensitive to social change.[3]

Pools and Pathways

The bottom line of church growth is determined by neither the vigor nor the sincerity with which ministry efforts are conducted nor the number of decisions being made. Instead, it is determined by the number of unchurched people who are being brought into established congregations. People-flow strategies can assist this process, an examination of which follows.

People Flow: Front-Door and Side-Door Models

I (Dan) developed the Front Door, Side Door People-Flow Model as I was working simultaneously on my Doctorate of Missiology in Fuller Seminary's School of World Mission and in consultation ministry at the Fuller Institute. It posits the theory that people come into our churches and become members not just by walking into our Sunday morning services (Front Door). A significant number of people start coming to the church through the "side door." Who makes their way through the "side door"? People who were first met in the community. They have been introduced to Christ or the church through neighborhood Bible studies, in justice or compassionate ministry efforts, in park or storefront ministries, or personal evangelism of all kinds. Some churches focus mostly on Front-Door Strategies, others on Side-Door Strategies. Yet others use a combination of both.

Front-door churches prefer to plan events that will draw non-Christians into the Christian influence. Side-door churches have become restless waiting for the lost and broken people to find a way to church. They believe that the message can best be understood in an atmosphere that is nonthreatening to unbelievers. This demands that Christians take the initiative in living out an authentic gospel in word and deed on their own home ground. Side-door approaches include a wide spectrum of activities, such as tent meetings in parks, canvassing door to door in cities, establishing storefront missions in slum neighborhoods, or developing after-hours Christian clubs at high schools.

Front-Door Fishing Pools

Front-door strategies can be grouped into four primary fishing pools, each representing scores of specific strategies with different labels and intended audiences. Each pool contains dozens of people with particular spiritual needs. Because fish swim at different depths, are attracted to different kinds of nourishment, and are hungry at different times, each pool requires a unique approach.

1. *Word-of-mouth churches* concentrate on developing an image of excitement or importance. They place regular articles in the newspapers or ads in theaters; their Web sites are among the most active. Sometimes excitement is generated simply by one person telling a neighbor or friend about his or her pastor or a certain activity in the church that has influenced that person's life. Other people then become curious enough to want to visit the church. Many non-Christians voluntarily choose to attend a service simply because they've heard from other "excited, contagious Christians."

2. *High-visibility events* are held within the walls of a church and are designed to meet a single need of one particular group of people. Depending on the circumstances, this might include a speaking appearance by an athlete, a congressman, a psychologist, an entertainer, or any other spokesperson with high credibility among a certain "microculture" or constituency.

3. *"Open" new residents* are looking for meaning and purpose, maybe after having broken ties with old friends and old lifestyles. Churches that understand this need and respond appropriately assimilate new people through this pool year-round. Sometimes this involves a combination

of introductory letters, telephone calls, and personal visits. In twenty-first-century settings, this may simply be multiple genuine, attentive touches by numerous worshippers over a period of weeks and months.

4. *"Andrew" invitations* are given to friends and associates. These invitations can be distinguished from word-of-mouth contacts by the guest's walking through the front door with a regular member of the congregation. Sometimes bringing in the guest involves a prayer strategy by which members are encouraged to pray for specific individuals and attempt to bring at least one person to a worship service during the year. Although personal invitations are still the most popular approach, they may not be the most suitable for every church. But in many cases, because of habit and tradition, this is the only outreach approach with which church leaders are familiar.

Once a person has walked through the front door, strategies for incorporating people into church congregations focus on processes more than events.[4]

Side-Door Fishing Pools

Many Americans will never enter the front door of a local church except for marriage or funeral services. Nevertheless, such individuals often have sincere needs that can best be ministered to by the Christian message. Growing churches using side-door approaches have discovered ways to meet these needs, win a relatively high percentage of these people to Christ, and incorporate them into the fellowship of the body. Congregations that "fish" thus are classified as side-door churches. Four primary sources of contacts have been identified, but they represent literally hundreds of specific methods.

1. *Community classics* are large events held in neutral auditoriums. They are distinguished from high-visibility

events merely by their location outside the walls of the church. Extensive neighborhood outreach campaigns are included in this category. The local church does not need to be the only vehicle that sponsors and develops these types of events in an outside auditorium. Key individuals in the church could simply open up their homes and invite their friends in for group meetings on a smaller scale.

2. *Community and affiliation activities* are smaller in scope than community classics and are designed to meet the isolated needs of people within a single homogenous unit. For one church it might be a motorcycle club for twenty-somethings; for another church it might include aerobics classes or a diet network for overeaters. Through connections to people who are associated with a single church, other individuals are one step closer to the church.

   Take, for instance, a weight counseling clinic for young mothers. Some churches will opt to hold this clinic in the community and will advertise it by putting posters in such places as laundromats, baby stores, and Christian bookstores. When the mothers gather for the meeting, they meet other young mothers their same ages who are outstanding, loving, friendly Christians. They greet and welcome the guests and pick individual guests to befriend during the time. One Christian lady who is an authority on weight control presents a program. She might naturally make a reference to her faith or her church during the presentation. During this seminar, relationships will build through small-group interaction. Some of the Christian mothers will invite the non-Christians into their homes during the week. They come together initially around a mutual need and in the process form other relationships. This outreach helps bring new people into the body of Christ.

3. *Personal contacts* are receptive individuals met within the course of a normal week. Lay leaders are trained to sense

spiritual needs in others with whom they come in contact at work, at home, at a shopping center, or at sporting events. Through these relationships, lay people have a direct role in leading others to a new life in Christ and fellowship in the local church.

4. *Friends of new Christians* are often receptive to the witness of a peer who has recently found Christ. When new Christians have been functioning within a local church for more than a year, close ties with non-Christians outside the church tend to disappear. Therefore, some growing churches specialize in training friendly and articulate Christians to meet the friends of new Christians and begin discipling each social network out to its fringe.

Side-Door Catching and Cleaning

A proverb states, "One must catch a fish before one can clean it." The same is true about non-Christians: catch them, then clean them. Although the exact process varies, discipling usually consists of five elements: personal evangelism, motivation for further involvement, establishment of personal relationships, involvement in small-group dynamics, and introduction to Christian fellowship.[5]

Side-Door and Front-Door Discipling

Side-door churches with evidence of steady growth have developed ongoing evangelism strategies in the community and ongoing maturation strategies in the church. On the other hand, front-door churches can evangelize and mature their communities only after non-Christians have entered the worship service. Consequently, their evangelism and maturing objectives are made exclusively among internal activities.

Growing churches arrange their activities according to levels of involvement and commitment. In the worship service, for example, the primary purpose is to strengthen the vertical relationship between God and the community who gather to worship. At a second level, fellowship groupings—such as men's or women's gatherings—fulfill the human need to belong. At still deeper levels, support and friendship structures, such as in small groups, provide greater receptivity for learning from and sharpening one another. The highest level of relationships, fulfillment, and personal growth occur when members are involved in missional teams.

A Multientry Church

Multientry churches have learned to create numerous avenues for the unchurched to enter through both the front door and the side door. Separate systems of catching and caring respond to the distinctive needs of front-door and side-door people. In addition to monitoring the flow of people and activities, church leaders also attend to the selection and training of new leaders for both front-door and side-door discipling activities. Many churches today should be encouraged to become a multientry church. Too many churches have become safe harbors for the convinced who have lost contact with the unconvinced. It's important, therefore, that some people flow out of the church doors and into the community.

Examples of Front-Door and Side-Door Churches

Robert Schuller and Bill Hybels were the pioneers in front-door discipling during the last generation of churches. Most of the side-door churches were smaller and less visible, many of them participating in the house-church movement. Among the most advanced churches in the new millennium, two stand out: Mosaic in Los Angeles and New Hope in O'ahu. Both of these congregations are excellent in their pace and process of reaching urban, postmodern people in large metropolitan areas. They both do so through forming and reproducing missional teams. Their strategies, however, are quite different. New Hope draws un-

churched persons through the front door with a simple contagious "you've-got-to-come-to-my-church" approach. The church
is also an integral part of its community, which makes people
want to come to the church.

Mosaic, on the other hand, is harder to find. While both
churches worship in rented facilities, Mosaic sometimes doesn't
know if it will be meeting in the same facility next week. It mul-
tiplies its ministry, however, through more than one hundred
LifeGroups that meet unchurched people on their own turfs and
engage them in life discussions. Both congregations draw persons from a wide geographical range and use multiple sites and
services, but their initial points of contact with unchurched persons is somewhat different. Both have evolved into a multientry
status, which means they also have missional teams doing both
front-door and side-door discipling. Still, New Hope tends to be
primarily a front-door church, with secondary side-door strategies, whereas Mosaic is primarily a side-door church with secondary front-door approaches.

Refinements

Several additional factors relate to people flow. Understanding them will help in selecting specific strategy combinations
that are right for your particular church.

Appropriate Balance

Because of the wide range of acceptable ministry options in
America, there is no "ideal" model. No two congregations are
the same, and if they could all be covered by one model, that
ideal would be impossible to achieve.

A common tendency is to favor just one pathway and to believe that the others are inferior. Such reasoning, however, is il-
logical. Common sense dictates that the more approaches used,
the greater the odds for finding a way for reaching out to more
people.

Front-door and side-door strategies are not synonymous with "come-and-go" philosophies, "gathering and scattering," or "inside-the-walls-versus-outside-the-walls" approaches. The multientry model presented in this chapter is unique in its identification of the context of the initial contact. Strategies labeled "go," "scattering," or "outside the wall" are often, in fact, nothing more than front-door strategies; they call for visiting people who've already attended a worship service. *Side-door audiences are different from front-door audiences in that they do not voluntarily attend church.* Although their spiritual receptivity may be high, their levels of awareness and commitment to church are often quite low. This is particularly true among people in their twenties. George Barna reports that people in this group consider themselves as being highly spiritual or interested in spiritual things, but as being unlikely to go to church. Conversely, senior citizens report themselves as being not particularly interested in spiritual things, but they are likely to go to church.

Advantages of Front-Door and Side-Door Churches

Congregations that have generated substantial centripetal forces (bringing people in through the front door) are able to minister quickly and efficiently. Central operations are easier to manage than those churches that are decentralized. Such advantages are sometimes offset, however, by inherent tendencies toward a slower ability to change, a false sense of faithfulness, and becoming overly dependent on architectural evangelism.

In side-door churches, on the other hand, centrifugal strategies are more effective in smaller churches where there's greater freedom for adaptability and assertiveness. Not all pastors have been called to lead large front-door pulpit ministries. Some pastors are, in fact, deliberately keeping a small-church feel while maintaining a large-church mentality. This is particularly true in the multisite churches that will develop another site when their church attendance reaches about five hundred. Some side-door churches are less formal and less conventional. Their language is usually more esoteric and includes more high-impact concepts. They often perceive themselves as being more countercultural and out of the mainstream. They're also able to reformulate old meanings and to present them in more relevant ways. In addition, side-door churches have the advantage of recruiting the unchurched to a cause or a group, rather than simply to an institution.

One common danger of side-door churches is the tendency to load their initial presentations of the gospel with too much ethical content. In such cases, members are led to a salvation by works, and an acceptance that is overly dependent upon performance. Side-door churches are often criticized, usually unjustly, for their excessive evangelism. In contrast with many popular theories, evangelism leads to fellowship more often than fellowship leads to evangelism.

People-Flow Examples

The last few years have witnessed a rapid increase in the development of practical people-flow strategies, ranging from conventional approaches (such as busing or television advertisements) to more innovative ideas (including "season ticket" strategies). A great deal of work, however, is involved in preparation and in following through on any particular plan. The "iceberg principle" states that 10 percent of effective evangelism time requires 45 percent preparation and 45 percent preservation. Also, at least two to three years, in general, is required to design and refine a new evangelistic strategy. Often, churches conclude prematurely that an approach is just not working. Such judgments are not valid until an idea has been properly installed and improved upon for at least a couple of years.

Over the long term, it's wise for a congregation not to limit itself simply to one or two fishing pools. Conditions can easily change, and some pools may soon become "fished out." Better strategies and greater growth potential can be realized by building a broader-based, more active, more intentional people-flow system. Such a system is often a fortunate, automatic development of effective ministry. As currents are identified, other ideas and resources for fishing tend to emerge naturally rather than in an artificial or contrived manner. Sometimes, for example, it's helpful to distinguish between fishing pools in the community and incorporation pools in the congregation. Although both types might be held in homes, they are conducted for different reasons and for different kinds of persons. A third fishing pool may take on a more assertive style of evangelism. In this latter setting, more than any other, new evangelists are identified and equipped.

When it's time to identify new fishing pools, those pools should be based on relationship ties and other commonalties rather than on arbitrary criteria. Leaders rise to the top quickly in settings in which the mixture of enthusiasm is strong and contagious. In front-door churches, involvement in people-flow activities begins at a low level and increases gradually. Attrition is typically high. Side-door churches require high levels of commitment right from the start. It is then quite common for commitment levels to taper off only slightly during the first few years. In both kinds of churches, the degree to which people will stay, learn, and minister correlates highly with the authenticity of the lives of believers who are there and the contagiousness of love of Christ that permeates the culture of the church. No amount of good programs and strategies can transform lives regularly if these qualities do not exist.

Sodality Structures

A final refinement in dual-pathway thinking—that is, utilizing both side-door and front-door strategies—comes from reflecting upon the movement of Christianity throughout history. As mentioned in the previous chapter, Ralph Winter has brought to the attention of the missionary world the fact of God's redemptive purpose having included two complementary structures—modality and sodality. In our experience, many churches are confused by and therefore nonsupportive of sodalities such as parachurch movements. Because of theological reasons or differences in style, some churches are often annoyed by the aggressiveness of sodality leaders. Churches can also be threatened by exhortations of sodality leaders to be more evangelistic or fearful of church members being mobilized in some captivating parachurch cause.

Yet, in studying the role of sodalities in evangelism, one can make several points in their favor. First, their ability to attract the unchurched and to incorporate new Christians is usually superior to the ability of modal, churchly structures. Second, although their existence has created tension for churches throughout the ages, sodalities are not an aberration but a complementary biblical vehicle for reaching non-Christians. Third, cooperation between local churches and local parachurch sodalities is essential in view of the daunting challenge of city transformation and in developing a kingdom perspective that cares for and equips new disciples.

Parachurch organizations ought not to be resented or considered second class. They ought not to be seen as competing but completing the kingdom work of the body of Christ. God raises up both the local church and the parachurch. The two can work well together if both understand the strengths and weaknesses of the other and allow mutual freedom.

If a local church will simply appreciate the work of these parachurch organizations—through seeking to meet the needs of sodality leaders; by supporting their work through prayer, finances, and public proclamation; and by helping to develop mutual strategies that will empower the productive evangelism and small-group discipleship of these ministries—then God will bless both units mightily. Further, the parachurch leaders must support the local church through prayer and a demonstration of commitment to the leadership of the church. This can be done by giving a portion of their finances to the church, attending the key services and meetings, communicating appreciation orally, and getting involved in a specific ministry in that church.

Questions to Consider

1. Is your church a "front-door" or a "side-door" church?
2. How are people coming into and leaving your church?
3. Do you have an intentional system for attracting, assimilating, and building up new people?
4. Where is your church strong in its people flow? Where is it weakest? How can you begin to develop a better people-flow system?

Case Study 6

People-Flow Strategy:
Erwin McManus, Mosaic Southern Baptist
Los Angeles, California

When Erwin walked in, I (Dan) knew there was something different about him. He was, in fact, quite different from anyone else in the room. I first saw him on the second day of the Council on Ecclesiology in Escondido, California, March 2001. A heated discussion was underway on the compromised church.

Everyone else was white or black, or from some distinct theological tradition. Erwin seemed to size us up—as well as our first day's thinking—a little too quickly. He was obviously not impressed with our conclusions. He saw things differently than anyone else in the room. Key people were in attendance from *Christianity Today*, World Vision, Willow Creek, Asbury Seminary, Dallas Seminary, Fuller Seminary, and the National Association of Evangelicals. We even had some of his best fellow Southern Baptists in the room! So how could he think so differently?

As I got to meet Erwin's leadership team at Mosaic up close during the next couple of years, I learned just how uniquely God has wired and prepared Erwin as a prophetic leader for such a time as this. Since that time he has dictated (normal people write) the most impressive trilogy on team building and ecclesiology in my entire library. Further, his leadership teams have reproduced themselves in as difficult a spot in America as exists— California—from UCLA to Pasadena's Rose Bowl to USC's Coliseum and throughout the vast San Gabriel and San Fernando valleys. These ethnically diverse, rapidly changing communities have thwarted the strategies of pastors and consultants since Billy Graham launched his famous crusade in 1948.

Although several megaministries have emerged in this terrain, few have been able to overcome the multicultural and other contextual barriers. Few, until the emergence of Mosaic, have been able to reach out to the Los Angeles metro area—a diverse population—in a significant manner. Mosaic's frontline disciples and leaders routinely unpack worldviews among the potential pools as though doing so were the norm among Christian churches. They continue to communicate compellingly with diverse worldviews in more than a hundred LifeGroups spread throughout the Los Angeles basin.

Erwin's team had to overcome additional difficulties. One was transitioning from the plateaued ministry of a beloved founding pastor who had a very defined philosophy of ministry. Second, Mosaic operated from a land-locked piece of property. Against all odds and all the previous rules of growth, within a short time Erwin's team had changed the name of the church, all of its core values, and were seeing rapid people flow through both the front and side doors in multiple locations. Their cross-cultural ministry is the most advanced I have seen in any missiological circle.

Another factor in Mosaic's exceptional capacity to reproduce new leaders is their innate ability to ask for *radical commitment* and to turn on a dime as the occasion of mission calls for it. The leadership team at Mosaic, for example, does not have to work at getting out of an institutional box like most congregations do. Creativity oozes from every pore. During one leadership retreat with several hundred of Mosaic's young leaders, their entire ministry went through a metamorphosis in a matter of minutes without chaos or confusion. The leadership dispensed with traditional membership and instead called all those who were fully behind the Mosaic vision "staff" as a recognition that they were shoulder to shoulder with the paid staff in the mission of the church.

Mosaic is a coalescing global force with creativity as its flaming, indefinable core. A second-generation textbook of people flow is in the process of being written. And all of Christianity is breathlessly watching.

9

Life-Giving System 7: Lifestyle Evangelism

One of the classic stories told in church growth lore involves a young cocktail waitress who accepted Christ as her Lord and Savior. While the young lady was receiving instruction for her upcoming baptism, the pastor suggested that she invite some of her friends from the bar where she worked to attend her baptism. The idea sounded good to her, and she followed through by sending personal invitations to many of the people she worked with at the local bar. On the evening of her baptism, three whole pews were filled with her friends. Just before she was baptized, they all heard her share how she received Christ as her Savior. Over the following twelve months, fifteen of her co-workers and friends also came to faith in Christ and were baptized in her church. During the second year, however, only five of her friends accepted Christ, and by the third year none of her co-workers or friends came to Christ.

This story illustrates that the more people get involved in church, and the more committed they become, the fewer friends they have outside that circle of faith. Before the young cocktail waitress received Christ, her circle of friends was composed primarily of others who also did not believe in Christ. When she became a believer in Christ, she had a group of friends to whom she could share her newfound faith. As the years went by, and she became more involved in the church, her circle of friends outside the church grew ever smaller. By the third year, she was so involved in church activities that her connection to people outside the church was gone. (This natural process is illustrated in fig. 9.1).

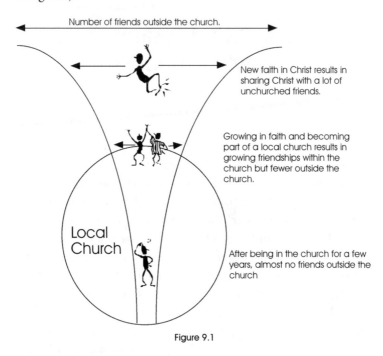

Figure 9.1

Without an intentional emphasis on outreach, even new Christians will soon become inward focused and have no meaningful contact with the unchurched people around them. It is essential that a church keep on training members to keep making new unchurched friends. Studies have discovered that in declining churches the worship attendees normally have fewer than four unchurched friends or family members. In plateaued churches the average is six unchurched friends per worshiper. But in growing churches, the members have nearly twelve unchurched friends. The more unchurched contacts that church members have, the greater the growth potential.

Developing an Outreach Strategy

Three skills should be stressed in training church members to reach out to unchurched friends and family members. The first skill focuses on where to meet prospective friends and how to go about establishing a genuine two-way relationship. The second deals with how to identify receptive people, be sensitive to their needs, and respond naturally and quickly when difficulties come into their lives. The third skill concentrates on knowing the church's resources for responding to the friend's need, and how to effectively invite the friend to meet with a person or attend an event that is a potential source of help.

Without an intentional team-based strategy that identifies and empowers individuals for lifestyle evangelism, very little of it is likely to occur. Thus, it is essential that a church develop an overall strategy that trains people in the previously mentioned skills. Most churches use a strategy that incorporates four levels of training (see fig. 9.2).

Level one focuses on serving people who are outside Christ and the church. At this level, churches that are effective in reaching their communities for Christ often build bridges of kindness into the community, providing food for those in need, helping single moms or dads provide holiday cheer for their families, or connecting with the aged and lonely. By serving the community in various ways, the church demonstrates a caring attitude that draws unchurched people toward Christ and the church. These ministries also help train church members to love those outside the church, as well as teaching them how to engage in conversation with unbelievers in a nonthreatening and natural manner.[1]

Level two focuses on inviting unchurched people to various events where they can be casually introduced to the church and to Christ. A church may offer a number of different events for this purpose: concerts, plays, picnics, twelve-step classes, children's programs, sports activities. At this level, church members are trained simply to invite their non-Christian friends and family members to attend an event for enjoyment or learning.

Figure 9.2

Level three focuses on making friendships at a deeper level. Church members are often encouraged to make a list of their non-Christian friends and family members. Once the list is made, they begin praying regularly for each person on their list. Members receive training on how to share their faith verbally with the people on their list. At this level, lifestyle or friendship evangelism approaches are most useful.[2]

Level four focuses on training church members who demonstrate great effectiveness in bringing newcomers to Christ. At this level, church members are often trained in more direct, confrontational styles of evangelism.

Churches that excel in equipping members to establish relationships with unchurched persons offer ongoing, practical training such as case studies and role-playing to reinforce the skills. Members should also be given frequent opportunities to hear the stories of those who are witnessing as a way of life. People who have been folded into the church through lifestyle evangelism are also encouraged to tell their stories. If a people-flow strategy is functioning effectively along with the other life-giving systems, a church will have many people who have become new Christians during the last two or three years. These "exhibit A's" will not only encourage the church but also be key indicators of the strategies that are working best.

Using Boundary Spanners

One resource often overlooked by churches is people who are on the fringe of a ministry, perhaps misunderstood and lacking affirmation, who have a special ability to maintain positive relationships with unchurched persons. These people are Boundary-Spanning Individuals (BSIs). They feel at home with both church friends and unchurched people, and they can "span the boundaries" that separate Christians and non-Christians. They are excellent people to involve in lifestyle evangelism and other ministries to non-Christians. Look for those who seem to be comfortable with both Christians and non-Christians, then involve them in the four levels noted earlier.[3]

Welcoming Teams

New Hope O'ahu, understands the importance of first impressions in communicating the heart and soul of the church. Anyone visiting the Saturday and Sunday services, which are set up and held each week in a local school, will feel welcomed and loved from the moment they step out of their cars. New Hope has put a high priority on creating welcoming teams composed of people whom visitors meet first. These people are gifted with hospitality and extend a friendly, gracious welcome. New Hope, in fact, places so high a priority on hospitality skills that they hire staff to help fill these roles. At least three full-time people meet and greet at each of their five weekly services and graciously follow up on scores of new contacts each week. This function is so critical to the people-flow process at New Hope, that church leaders are very selective in who becomes part of these numerous welcoming teams.

All too often, greeting and "ushering" is often seen as an entry-level ministry, or a place to serve for those who are past their primes or cannot be placed in other ministries. Greeting, however, is a specialized and vital ministry that may make a difference in whether people go out "the back door" and never return or stay for several years. This area of ministry is far too important to be left to chance. Thus, an intentional strategy is required for this critical element, and advanced, specialized training is essential for these welcoming teams.

Learning to Fish

In life outside the church, harvesting and fishing are fascinating to observe. As in most endeavors, gifted and seasoned professionals make it look easy, whereas amateurs, though often enjoying themselves, lack precision and perspective. The same pattern can be observed in harvesting and fishing in churches. Most common errors made by congregations attempting to establish effective lifestyle and other evangelism strategies can be grouped according to four categories: process, people, attitude, balance.

Process

Many event-driven evangelism strategies fail because they emphasize isolated events and programs. Often when churches prepare an outreach event, too little thought is given to appropriate follow-up activities. Will guests be identified, for example, during the event? If so, how and when will it be done, and what will happen after they've been identified? If guests are not identified during the event, what kind of follow-up is realistic? Also, it is usually best to develop a series of events over a period of a year or two, rather than plan just a single event. By holding several events within a short period of time, the process of preparation, conducting the event, and follow-up can be refined after each of the first two attempts. It's also recommended that the same team be responsible for both planning and evaluating all of these events. This team can decide what adjustments should be made after each event, and can track how many new disciples are now involved in small groups or team activities as a result of initial contacts at these events.

People

In some instances, the process for increased health and growth is sound, but the workers have not been properly selected and placed. Even with thorough training, certain tasks cannot be carried out effectively. Giftedness is especially important in evangelism. Although everyone can improve in personal witnessing, those chosen to lead the operation must have intuitive abilities. Without such persons, the authentic message and ministry of a congregation often fails to match the needs of the unchurched. Those who witness effectively generally do so within their own sphere of influence.

Frequently overlooked factors in the selection of people are the use of language, lifestyle, and location. Neighbors often are defined as those within certain geographical boundaries—and especially those next door. In most communities, though, neighborhoods in the traditional sense no longer exist. Instead, people "neighbor" according to vocation, recreation, and education they share in common.

Attitudes

Even with the right people in the right place using the right process, strategies can fail. Two improper attitudes are frequently the cause: unconscious insensitivity and unintentional exclusiveness. Invisible signs—ones that only visitors see—say "take us or leave us" or simply "keep out." Sometimes a "no" response from a newcomer does not always mean no; it may, however, require persistence and creativity before it becomes a "yes."

Balance

Some churches are not growing in spite of a steady flow of persons through the front door and several side doors as well. The difficulty lies in the size of the "back door"—more people are leaving than are arriving. The reasons these members, including leaders, express for leaving are not always the real reasons. Thus, as much effort should be put into discovering the causes for such departures as is put into encouraging new arrivals.

It can be assumed that unless people are encouraged to become more than Sunday morning attendees, they will not become part of the church community and its ministry. Effective strategies require front and side doors that are wide open, and back doors that are reserved for only legitimate "emergencies."

Blessability Factor

Over the years, we have worked with a number of congregations that, in spite of doing everything right, did not show any measurable increase. What accounts for this lack of growth? There are two possibilities. First, some unidentified factor may be retarding or inhibiting growth. Sometimes it may take years to discover this factor. In several cases, for example, a breakdown in the relationship between two staff members had an adverse effect on momentum. No one except the two individuals were aware of what was going on "behind the curtain." In other cases, the pastor's marriage was in trouble, or some kind of secret sin was later discovered that explained why the pastor was not able to provide the necessary 100 percent commitment.

Second, it is possible that, in the mystery of God's value system, He may have chosen, at least up until now, to withhold His blessing. It cannot always be explained why one congregation makes growth look so easy, and a second one, even one on the same street, struggles for years. The second church has had to overcome one obstacle after another to find a combination for fruitfulness, but with little or no evidence of God's blessing.

Other mysteries of blessing, too, cannot be explained, such as why one pastor has ten talents and another must be content with only two or three talents. This kind of comparison often leads to discouragement and envy, allowing the growth of a cynical and pessimistic attitude.

We as Christians are commanded to make disciples. As we yearn for growth, let us do all we humanly can to partner with God toward maximum fruitfulness.

Questions to Consider

1. What might be the result if your church were able to double or triple the number of people who have been assimilated through all of the friendship-making and overall ministry activities?
2. What kind of positive impact would such an increase have on the ability of the congregation to fulfill its mission?
3. How much of a difference would such growth make to morale and to the momentum of your ministry?
4. What plan or strategy do you currently use to develop the evangelistic effectiveness in your church? What needs to be improved?

Case Study 7

Lifestyle Evangelism:
New Hope Christian Fellowship O'ahu
Honolulu, Hawaii

Without a doubt New Hope O'ahu is the most intentionally and effectively evangelistic church I (Dan) have come across in North America. Evangelism permeates the DNA of every leader, yet not in the conventional sense of evangelistic outreach and strategies. Most of the believers at New Hope have been so radically transformed that their lives are simply contagious. Team members see their roles as critical to, and directly related to, winning the lost. Each team member views his or her ministry role—whether it be sound tech, raking leaves, praying over the seats of people who will attend services—as just as important to the overall task of reaching a soul as those who are up front in a more visible role of communicating the gospel.

All team members are in groups that feed regularly on God's Word. Thus, they are so alive in Christ that they're very comfortable with talking in natural ways with those around them about what they're learning. They're also just as comfortable in inviting their friends and family members to come to New Hope for a weekend service. Inviting is, in fact, what every member seems to do very simply and effectively. With great enthusiasm, they simply say, "You've got to come to my church. Just try it one time. I know you'll like it, just like I did." And for many invitees, that's all it takes.

Even people who do not attend New Hope are aware of their intention to have a positive impact on the entire island of O'ahu. Most nonmembers whom I've spoken with are favorably impressed. Residents of the island see New Hope people daily reading their Bibles at the beach and at Starbucks. Additionally, New Hope ministers in their city in practical, loving, and generous ways. One of New Hope's goals is for people in O'ahu—whether or not church members, believers or not in Jesus—to say, "I want New Hope to stay in our community because. . . ."

The church performs numerous community-related activities such as giving school supplies to children as they begin school, providing computers, and renovating school classrooms. Nonmembers also hear multiple stories of people in their workplace whose lives have been positively transformed because of the influence of New Hope. Everything they do is consistent with their core values. So when a resident of O'ahu has a crisis in life or begins to think about God, one of the first places they are likely to think about is New Hope—and New Hope is prepared.

10

Life-Giving System 8: Charting the Future

A few years ago, I (Gary) consulted with a church that had recently experienced a pastoral change. The staff members of this larger church were extremely frustrated with the new pastor. After several interviews with each staff person, I discovered that the basic issues involved mapping the future. The previous pastor had taken a hands-on approach in working with each staff member to develop a common direction for the future of not only the entire church but also each team member's specific ministry. The new pastor, however, took a dim view of planning. He thought that the church and community were changing too quickly to make planning worthwhile. Thus, the only direction he gave the staff was, "Just do your jobs." The staff members were struggling to understand the overall mission, vision, and goals for the church under the new senior pastor's nonplanning approach.

Planning efforts today are much more challenging than in the past because of the sheer number of changes as well as speed at which changes are occurring in the church and society. Congregational planners traditionally assumed that most changes would be both gradual and predictable. The unprecedented societal shifts noted earlier, however, might cause many congregational leaders to conclude that attempts to project the future are no longer worth the effort.[1] At the opposite end of the spectrum are those leaders who insist that not only is planning essential but also that all staffing, programs, facilities, and finances must have five- to ten-year detailed projections.

Figure 10.1

It is best to avoid either of these extremes. Churches obviously cannot afford to abandon planning altogether or to be bound by obsolete and overly rigid approaches. Instead, future-mapping approaches must be dynamic and interactive. It must be assumed that rapid and tumultuous changes are normal, that the pace and magnitude of change overall may well increase, and that mapping must occur through interrelations with and interdependence on other life-giving systems.[2] Planning can easily become mechanical, sterile, and carnal if, for example, it is not undergirded and prepared for by corporate intercession or if it ignores the demands of people flow.

Visionary Mapping

A number of recent books, conferences, and periodicals point out the connection between visionary mapping and effective ministry. And rightly so. Vision has been energizing successful missions and ministries throughout biblical and contemporary history.

Three Proven Phases

Although the world is changing dramatically, mapping the future can continue to build upon the three proven phases of planning: assessing trends, determining direction, and implementing strategies. In some instances, it will be necessary to find language that is more suitable to a denominational heritage or to the microcultures a church is seeking to infiltrate with the gospel. In some cases, it will also be necessary to break these three phases into additional categories. But, overall, these three phases can be used effectively for most mapping projections with each phase being given as much detail as deemed necessary by the mapping participants.

Some mapping teams require more detailing of sequences than others. For example, is the process confusing? More clarification is necessary. Is the process bogging down in minutiae? Try to combine or eliminate certain mapping tasks.

A Short Time Frame

For most congregations, a time frame of several months is adequate to complete an initial map. If the mapping period goes beyond nine months, the overall impact likely will be diminished. In other words, don't get consumed by the planning process. A clear point of diminishing returns will occur at which the planning begins to lose momentum. For the sake of the congregation, it's imperative that the mapping process culminate in a

crescendo, not in a gasp of exhaustion. Ai
ends in celebration and exhilaration, not o
boredom and burnout.

Congregations become weary of a planni
bogged down. The "world record" for leng
logged by a mainline group in the San Francisco Bay area with
whom I (Dan) consulted about a decade ago. They'd been meeting continuously for eight years, working on their long-range
plan. When I was in the area a few years later, I called them to ask
how things were going. They said, "Things are going fine, and
we're still enjoying the process as much as ever!" The group was
misnamed as a planning group. It had been meeting primarily
for fellowship and pie, rather than for serious mapping, and had
done none of the implementation I'd discussed with them. The
group was more comfortable thinking about doing something
than doing it.

Focus on the Basics

Determining future direction is best accomplished by focusing on four basics: mission, values, vision, and goals. Written
surveys and on-site interviews are the best means to assess patterns and trends. In most cases some kind of data packet is also
completed with basic information on the congregation, the leadership, and the community.

Mission

What is mission? It's the biblical reason that a particular church
exists. Some people call this the "purpose" of the church. It really doesn't matter which term one uses as long as it's used con-
sistently. Although a church's mission statement may be worded
differently from time to time, it essentially never changes and
can never be accomplished completely.[3] Wayside Chapel in San
Antonio, Texas, for example, states its mission thus:

To glorify God by making disciples
who have a heart for God,
for one another,
and for the whole world.

As can be seen, this mission can never be accomplished fully. There will always be room for making disciples. There will always be a need to assist people in forming a heart for God, for one another, and for the whole world.

Values

What are values? They are the core beliefs of the church. Essentially, core values are what a church stands for or holds dear. They are the basic beliefs upon which churches make decisions. Many churches are finding that an effective way to express their values is by using the church name as an acrostic. Grace Church in LaVerne, California, for example, states their core values thus:

Genuine Christian Living
Reaching the Lost
Authentic Worship
Continuous Growth
Excellence in Ministry

Vision

What is vision? It's the big picture that a church believes God is leading them to accomplish. For Nehemiah, vision was rebuilding the walls of Jerusalem and moving the inhabitants of the city out of their shame and disgrace. For Paul, it was starting churches throughout the Roman Empire, filled with Gentile believers who were trusting Jesus for salvation. A shared vision is a unifying force that can unite constituents around a common pursuit, enabling them to accomplish together what they could only hope for as individuals.

To be effective, a congregational vision at any moment must be captivating, compelling, and comprehensive. The direction must be clear and specific. It must stretch and inspire the imagination, but it must also be obtainable and flexible. For example, Grace Church explained their vision thus:

> The vision of Grace Church is to
> relocate to a new campus within five years,
> build a new multipurpose facility,
> involve 50 percent of our people in using their gifts,
> and get 80 percent of our people into small groups.

Clearly, that is a vision that is captivating, compelling, and comprehensive.

Goals

What are goals? Goals are the measurable outcomes a church must accomplish to fulfill their vision during the next 3–5 years. Specific action steps must also be completed in order to clarify time frames and persons responsible for achieving each goal. Goals and action steps should be more detailed during the first two years. But beyond twelve to twenty-four months, congregational goals should not become overly detailed or limited in their options.

The entire package of mission, values, vision, and goals form a church's map for the future. A great deal has been learned about effectiveness in congregational mapping during the past decade. The process can range from a strong consultant-led approach to a primarily team-led approach, with the consultant coaching a team of lay leaders from behind the scenes. In most cases, it is highly desirable to introduce the map to the congregation at large, allowing sufficient time to establish a broad base of ownership among them for the vision and overall direction.

Pulsing the Congregation

One of the most valuable components in congregational mapping is the concept of taking the pulse of, or pulsing, various groups to understand their thoughts and feelings concerning the future direction. Figure 10.2 shows one way of pulsing a congregation for, in this example, developing a mission statement.

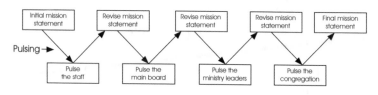

Figure 10.2

Include anyone who perceives himself or herself as having a "stake" in the future. Pulse group sessions may consist of groups of up to twenty-five people, or they may involve as few as three to five people. The facilitator listens to and records, *without editorial comment,* the responses of people to several strategic questions. By not editing or commenting on responses, an atmosphere of trust is established, and people know that their exact words and thoughts are valued; consequently, they are more open to share their perspective.

Sometimes it is valuable to have several rounds of pulsing, particularly when controversial issues that may affect a large percentage of the congregation must be worked through. When in doubt, it is better to err on the side of additional rather than fewer pulsing sessions to ensure open, honest, two-way communication between leaders and grassroots congregants. As one famous Southern preacher put it, "You got to keep your ears so close to the ground that you get them full of grasshoppers."

Several additional developments should have a significant impact upon future planning.

Contextual or Environmental Categories

One of these new developments in assisting congregations to chart their futures is the expansion of diagnostic categories and the availability of information in usable formats. Most people now are familiar with the diagnostic category of *demographics* and understand the need for mapping processes to be informed about the ethnicity, vocation, education, income, and so forth of groups and communities. Another category, *psychographics,* is now distinguished from its parent term, demographics. The field of psychographics examines and develops information on the "softer" and less easily assessed categories of beliefs and attitudes.

During the last decade, a third category of demographics has found its way into strategic mapping discussions for leadership teams. The origins of spiritual demographics, or *dynagraphics,* can be traced to the spiritual powers of darkness and light. We are increasingly learning to respect the spiritual histories of communities and of congregations as unique and significant. Whether Native American pagan temples or the more contemporary Satanists, certain communities have developed either a higher resistance or receptivity to the gospel because of the abundance or absence of certain spiritual practices. Years of effective and focused Christian intercession, for instance, is proving in some cities to be a significant factor in influencing various networks of unchurched peoples.

All of these demographic insights should be factored into a congregation's strategic mapping process. Indeed, in this technological age, these external information categories are accessible through CD-ROM in the form of attractive, affordable, and usable charts and computer-enhanced video presentations. Such innovations make the available information more alive and more likely to affect the strategic decisions of congregational leaders.

In this fast-changing world, it is good, of course, to keep taking a pulse on these different demographics. Often, a particular team may enjoy developing this type of information and can be given the task of doing so.

Microcultural Awareness

Leadership teams can no longer be inhibited about developing strategies aimed at particular groups of people. In some cases, a church's survival will depend on their having a working knowledge of emerging microcultures. Congregations that take seriously the Great Commission eventually will be burdened and drawn toward particular groups in their community and around the world. For missional teams, discerning and taking the pulse of such groups can be a helpful and a necessary component of strategic mapping and the focus of prayer and discussion. The apostle Paul said, "Therefore I run in such a way, as not without aim; I box in such a way, as not beating the air" (1 Cor. 9:26). Every congregation should be listening to God and seeking discernment about whom they are called to serve.

A particular mission and vision, if they are to be realized fully, cannot be arrived at unintentionally by a church and its leaders. Where does the church stand? Where is it heading? How will it get there? These are critical questions. Those who trust and are willing to follow godly leaders in a missional cause deserve to have answers to these questions. As Christian church members, our question, "For whom are we burdened?" does not arise from selfish desires but from a humble desire to act as missionaries, coming alongside particular peoples, to identify with their pain and misfortune, and to lay down our lives for their welfare and for matters that affect their eternal destiny.

Misperceptions About Culture

Along with the discovery of new microcultures will come the realization that culture is a much more important ingredient in strategic mapping than was previously realized. How do we as church members learn, for example, to separate our genuine Christian faith from our particular denomination's tradition and cultural trappings? How do we reclothe the gospel to remain faithful to our biblical doctrines and at the same time be relevant to those we are called to serve? Many congregational leaders have only an inkling of such missiological insights. American pastors and leadership teams need, as much as anyone, to see how concepts related to culture are essential to fulfilling their mission and for increasing their strategic impact in their community.

Finding and Establishing a Church's DNA

Today, many churches are ineffective because they attempt to find the "right" formula by borrowing it from some other group that claims to have the best approach. Leaders who have pioneered thriving ministries have shared their insights in seminars and workshops across the country. Thousands of preachers have attended, seeking to learn from these most "successful pastors and churches."

Finding a particular church's correct "formula," however, is a complex undertaking and one that can be extremely frustrating and disappointing for leadership teams. The best help usually consists, though, in a church becoming enabled and encouraged to discover its own unique shape and mission; "one size does not fit all." Valuable lessons can be learned from and great tools received from model churches, but it's important that a church finds and comes to understand its own identity.[4] It can then work on the means to accentuate that identity in more specific and creative ways.

Questions to Consider

1. How much more effective and faithful might your church be if it had a complete map of its future?
2. What first steps can you take to develop your church's mission, values, vision, and goals?
3. What must be done this year to get started?
4. For whom is your church burdened?

Case Study 8

Charting the Future:
Dave Ferguson, Community Christian Church,
Naperville, Illinois

Dave Ferguson and I (Dan) met several years ago during a gathering in the office of *Christianity Today.* Dave Travis of Leadership Network had invited Dave Ferguson and his team to present his new concept of multisite ministry to a group of us who serve on an ad hoc group known as the Church Champion's editorial board. Dave Ferguson's ideas about one church in more than one location clearly had some new twists.

Dave invited me to meet with his leaders for several sessions during the next year. I got to know their hearts, their vision, and the particular way they think. From the beginning they've worked as a team who are clear about their vision and passionate about its implementation. They understand who they are and what they are about. They have established their DNA, and many others are drawn to the clarity of their mission and the attractiveness of their teams. Clearly, Dave is being raised up by God as one of the new leaders of the emerging global church. In addition to being lead pastor at Community Christian Church, he is shaping a fast-moving multisite movement called "New Thing."

Dave is an exceptionally quick study. He's incorporated not only most of the best practices from the past but, more importantly, those innovations just beginning to be glimpsed from the future. It didn't hurt Dave to have Lyle Schaller living in his hometown, constantly encouraging him to try this thing called multisite. But Dave has much more going for him than just the dean of consultants living nearby. He knows how to chart the future in a way that very few pastors do. He's integrated the best of Wayne Cordeiro, Erwin McManus, and Randy Frazee, to mention just a few. Willow Creek and New Hope have also received innovative ideas from him that enabled them to seize their own futures more quickly.

I'll never forget how Troy, a big man and the largest member of Dave's team, almost knocked me over during our first session in his eagerness to ask me, "Can you show us how to go faster?" I don't recall ever having had a planning question phrased quite like that. The team under Dave's leadership has a high-speed mapping process that is as unobtrusive as breathing. They assess, then accelerate, assess again, and then accelerate even more.

11

Life-Giving System 9: Streamlining the Organization

I think our church is feeling old," said Mike Graves, a lifelong member of Prince of Peace Church.

"What do you mean?" asked Mary Price, who'd recently started regularly attending Prince of Peace.

"I don't mean our people are getting old," Mike said. "What I mean is our church seems like it's become inflexible. We just take too long to make decisions anymore."

"Tell me more," Mary urged. "I'm so new here I'm still not really sure what you mean."

"Well," Mike began, "in the early years of our church, we made decisions very fast. If someone had a new idea, we just seemed to go with it. Now, if a new idea is suggested, it has to pass through two or three committees for approval. By the time we approve a new idea, it's often too late to implement it."

"Yes, I think I understand what you're saying now," agreed Mary, closing her eyes as if thinking of something particular. "At our last women's missionary luncheon, some of the ladies were talking about the new initiative for short-term mission teams."

"What did they say?" Mike asked, leaning forward in his chair.

"They said that it took nearly fifteen months for the proposal to go through the missions committee, then the finance committee, and finally to the church board. By the time it was finally approved, the person who suggested the idea had become frustrated and left our church."

"That's what I mean!" Mike said, his voice rising. "That's what I mean. We're getting old."

Old and Young Churches

What makes a church old or young is not the length of time it's been in existence. Nor is it related to the ages of the people who attend its services. Rather, an old church is one that has difficulty adapting to change, that is, the church is inflexible, whereas a young church is one that adapts easily to change, that is, it is flexible.

As change affects a congregation, adjustments must be made to the internal organizational structures. The current structure may be at odds with installing and restructuring the life-giving systems, and some changes may be in order. At least one person—or, more ideally, a small team—should be assigned to investigate what adjustments should be made and to make recommendations for continuously improving the operations of the life-giving systems. That person or group could take four steps, explained below, to accomplish this goal.

Revisit Scriptural Principles of Organizational Structure

Scripture supports and demonstrates organizational structuring. Moses, for example, organized Israel into units of thousands, hundreds, fifties, and tens. Nehemiah deployed people, resources, and processes. Paul established principles regarding elders and deacons in the Gentile churches. Scripture does not decree that any one organizational structure is better than another, but it's clear that order, responsibility, and decision making need to be present, and that the members of the body should function according to their gifts.

Review the Purpose and Functioning of Organizational Structure

Another task involves defining purposes and goals that inform the church's current organizational structure, and seeing which parts of the structure no longer serve the vision and ministry of the church. The organizational structure should support and generate the ministry and enable the life-giving systems to grow and thrive. This means that the resources of the church should be examined to ensure that they're supporting the current priorities. These resources include not only funds and facilities but also other resources that have been identified in the life-giving systems, such as people's time, giftedness, and energy.

The value of structure is that it can channel the right resources to the right place at the right time to generate the right results. This process is often referred to as "alignment." The resources of manpower, money, management, and ministry of prayer must be aligned with the purposes of the church. Are the right people aligned in support of the church's mission, vision, and goals? Are the financial resources of the church aligned to support the purpose and functions of the church? Is the management structure of the church guiding or blocking the church's direction into the future? Is a team of intercessors aligned to pour their prayers into the accomplishment of the church's ministries?

Additionally, a streamlined church structure will clearly indicate where authority rests within the church, delineate acceptable guidelines for executing the mission, and establish lines of communication. These guidelines and lines of communication will be as clear and unencumbered as possible and will have accountability built into them.

Study the Principles That Are Shaping the Structures of Viable Twenty-First-Century Congregations

A third task is to become aware of principles that are shaping other viable twenty-first-century churches. First, in all effective organizations—including the church—mission and vision, not maintenance, are the driving force. The structure follows mission and is shaped and directed by it. In a mission-driven structure, the right people do the right tasks in the right places at the right times. Second, structures appropriate for the twenty-first century tend to be decentralized. Staff and volunteers are equipped and released for ministry. Where authority is released and permissions are given, where emerging leaders experiment with new strategies, that's where more leaders will be developed and more ministries will occur. When leaders decentralize tasks and communication, and when trust exists, new energy and effectiveness will be unleashed.

Hand in hand with decentralization and empowerment is the emergence of process teams. In the new structure, similar ministry processes are grouped together instead of fragmented. People come together to partner on tasks and become mission-directed teams that fulfill a specific mission and strategy. Collaboration within the team and with other teams can generate a synergy that is contagious and compelling.

Design an Appropriate Streamlining Strategy

The fourth task is designing an appropriate strategy to accomplish the task of organizational streamlining. This means defining a church's mission and vision and designing a structure that focuses on the life-giving systems as they relate to a particular church. Ministry descriptions and organizational charts should be kept as unencumbered as possible. Mission-directed teams, according to the life-giving systems framework, should be empowered to continue charting the direction in their respective areas. "Buy-in" to the benefits and value of the new structure should be secured from the majority of church membership and leaders, and minimal restrictions should be placed upon the teams. Trust and credibility are thereby earned.[1]

Two Approaches

One approach used successfully by churches to streamline their structure is "permission giving" (fig. 11.1). A congregation will elect its leaders (elders, deacons, senior pastor), for example, and then give them permission to establish the overall direction and policies of the church. The congregation essentially delegates its authority to the leadership board, becoming involved in the voting process only on large items such as the buying and selling of church property, the changing of the church constitution, and so forth. The exact arenas in which a congregation becomes involved vary from church to church. The basic idea, though, is that the congregation chooses its leaders and then trusts them to lead.

The leaders then give the senior pastor permission to hire the rest of the pastoral staff and to run the church daily within the policies and guidelines established by the primary board. Although the senior pastor is accountable to the main board, the running of the staff and the daily ministry decisions are left up to the pastoral staff. Few, if any, committees exist. Most decisions are handled directly by the leaders or the pastoral team members. Task-force teams are used, of course, as appropriate, but few standing committees or commissions are employed, keeping the decision-making structure simple.

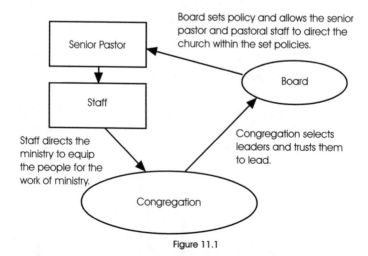

Figure 11.1

The pastoral staff then gives the people in the church permission to become involved in ministry based on their individual spiritual giftedness. Any suggestion for a ministry is an option as long as it is biblical, legal, moral, and fits within the overall charting of the church's direction. All ministries must, of course, fit within the doctrinal standards of the church.[2] This structure might look like the diagram in Figure 11.1.

Another approach that is gaining in understanding and popularity is called "fractaling," a term meaning "duplicating itself." New Hope Church in Hawaii is one example of this new approach to streamlining ministry. The core of this church's structure is built around the church's mission statement and is energized through team ministry. The church's mission is divided, for example, into four ministry objectives, or areas, that are viewed as extensions of the senior pastor's ministry. A person or couple is recruited to be responsible for each of the four areas of ministry (see fig. 11.2).

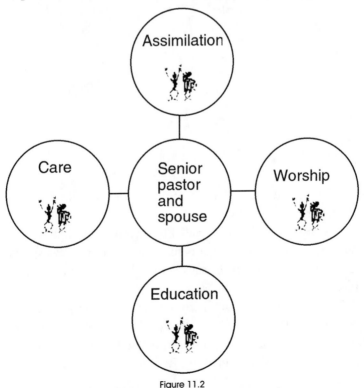

Figure 11.2

This team becomes a small group of up to ten people who work, pray, and plan together. Since the group has a built-in care-giving system, the members also minister to each other in appropriate ways.

Each of the four leaders in the outer circles develops a mission statement that fits his or her specific area of ministry. Then they recruit people to be responsible for each area of ministry. For example, see Figure 11.3.

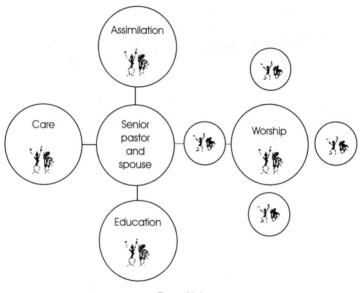

Figure 11.3

When all four areas of the mission statement are filled, it looks like Figure 11.4.

The process is simply repeated throughout the church, with each area of ministry being organized around four key aspects. As the system grows, it "fractals," or duplicates itself repeatedly. (See fig. 11.5.)

The fractaling approach to church structure offers at least five benefits. First, everyone is involved on a team. Second, everyone has a built-in small group for support and care. Third, a clear line of responsibility and authority is evident. Fourth, an ever-

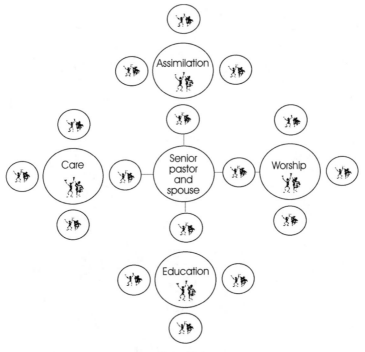

Figure 11.4

expanding network of ministry arises. Fifth, a predictable line of succession in leadership develops.[3]

Both of these approaches—permission giving and fractaling—offer new ways to structure a church for growth and health. It is not necessary, however, for a church to adopt one of these two approaches. It is only important that a church adopt a simpler structure of decision making so that it can adapt to change more quickly. Younger churches usually grow faster and easier than older churches. But churches can become young again, in part by streamlining their structures to be flexible and adaptable to change.

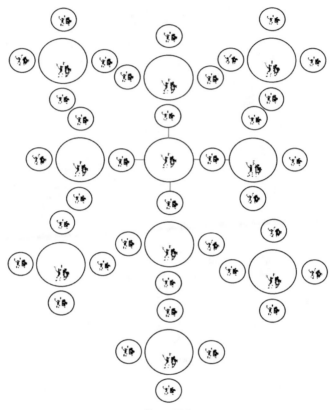

Figure 11.5

Questions to Consider

1. What might be the result if your church had an organizational structure with a minimum of bureaucratic constraints?
2. What would it take, on an ongoing basis, to remove any barriers that are preventing organizational streamlining and to generate an environment in which the life-giving systems could flourish and interact with one another?
3. Which of the two approaches to sreamlining church structure would best fit your church?
4. What is your church's DNA? How are you uniquely different from other churches?

Case Study 9

Streamlining the Organization:
Jon Beyer, Crosswinds Community Church (Reformed Church in America)
Canton, Michigan

Many pastors can relate to the dilemma in which Jon Beyer found himself a few years ago. He was spinning at least twenty-three ministry plates. Virtually all of his team members looked directly to Jon for pastoral care and coaching for their areas of responsibility. But like Moses, Jon was wearing himself out. When I (Dan) asked Jon if he wanted to shift to a plan that would relieve him from having so many of these responsibilities, he was ready and willing to trust the process. For most leaders in Jon's situation, however, the thought of letting go of control and plunging into the unfamiliar is simply too frightening.

The next month, Jon set up a weekend with his leadership team on Friday evening and all day Saturday. Our purpose was to help his team streamline their ministry through the fractaling-style approach developed at New Hope O'ahu. My wife and I helped them to identify four primary functions that would best enable them to extend Jon's ministry and accomplish their God-given mission as a church. All of Crosswinds' legitimate activities were placed in one of four "baskets." This process is similar to being asked to sort all files on a hard drive, but having only a choice of four folders. One must simply select the folder which best fits the particular file topic. Or one might delete a file if it no longer serves a valuable purpose, or combine two or more files under a new name.

Since that time they have formed new teams around these four areas, and leaders have emerged with some fresh ideas that have caused the Crosswinds vision to surge to a new level. Jon now has much more discretionary time to devote not only to those things that are in his area of gifting and passion in the church, but also to be with his family and to coach other churches in the Detroit area. Jon now has time to develop the training base he's dreamed about for years. Very likely, Crosswinds Community Church can now become a resource center for churches throughout Ohio and Michigan. Pastors caught in this common dilemma may want to take the same plunge as Jon did.

Life-Giving System 10:
Thriving on Change

Earlier in the book, the metaphor of a hot air balloon helped illustrate what might be holding a church back. I (Dan) have used this metaphor in my seminars and consultations for years, and I always ask the participants how many of them have experienced a ride in a hot air balloon, how many would like to, and how many would never even consider it. My wife, Ethelwynne, told me that if I asked those questions long enough someone would ask if I'd been in one. So on a vacation in Napa Valley, Ethelwynne and I decided to take a ride.

Very early one morning, with four other people, we squeezed into a basket. Attendants untied the ropes, and the pilot released the ballast and blasted hot air into the limp fabric. The hot air inflated the colorful balloon, and we took off. The ride was memorable. The view of the hills and vineyards was stunning, we were floating in a wicker basket hundreds of feet above the ground, and the hair on my arms was being singed by the propane blast. But the best was yet to come.

Within minutes of reaching our cruising altitude, the pilot told us that new weather conditions had developed. "If I'd known fifteen minutes earlier," he said, "it would've prevented our taking off!" We spent the rest of the trip looking for a place to set down because we weren't on course and weren't coordinating with the ground crew to be there when we arrived. We finally did set down, with a few bumps. We got to know the rest of the basket occupants a bit more intimately as we all fell on top of one another, tumbling out of the basket. It was fortunate, though, that none of us was any the worse for our journey, and we all have stories to tell to our friends and family—and readers of our books!

The story underscores, however, one other principle connected with this metaphor—that weather conditions are important. A good balloonist is prepared for changes in the weather and knows that smooth sailing is not guaranteed. In the culture and climate in which we find ourselves, things are, in fact, much more likely to be unpredictable than they have been in the past. Some prophetic voices say that we'd be wrong to expect safety and predictability. The world is a dangerous place and always has been for believers—check with the prophet Daniel and the apostle Paul. We must be ready to thrive in the middle of change, even danger.

Congregational leadership teams must come to grips with knowing that within their lifetimes the pace of change will continue to increase in all aspects of ministry. Rather than wait for the good old days to return, we all need to lean into these new realities by adjusting our attitudes and our modes of operation. In the majority of instances, new skills will be required. Thriving on change is a foundational skill for leadership teams in the new millennium. Whereas individuals have great difficulty surviving in a chaotic and highly turbulent environment, missional teams are at their very best when just about everything is unpredictable and uncontrollable.

Three Key Areas

Three key areas of change must be anticipated: increased mobility, increased diversity, and increased complexity. First, people will be increasingly mobile in both churches and communities. The incidence of people coming and going is, in fact, so high in some church communities that pastors feel that they're preaching to a parade. They must "catch them while they go by." While this may be helpful for initial evangelism, it's difficult to prepare people for future ministry in the church. If you as a church leader encounter this type of mobility in your church, then it has to figure into your strategy.

The diversity of churches is also increasing. In our experience, we find diversity in the kinds of people, in their preferences, in their backgrounds, and in their experiences. Much of the conflict found in churches is attributable to diversity. Take, for example, the struggle most churches experience in determining a style of worship. The diversity of preferences among the various generations found in the typical church is part of the cause.

Ministry is also becoming quite complex; factors produced by the societal changes cited in the introduction to this book are increasing the degree of difficulty for ministries to connect with people outside the church. Just one generation ago, many pastors oversaw a ministry that was quite simple. Fifty years ago, most churches offered one worship service, one Sunday school, a men's group, a women's group, and child care. Today, many churches offer multiple worship services; have reconfigured, revamped, and sometimes renamed Sunday school; provide various groups often too numerous to mention. Things are no longer simple.[1]

Some Implications

In addition to increasing complexity, two additional trends must also be recognized. Denominational loyalty and financial generosity are decreasing. What are the implications of these fundamental changes for the average church?

Foremost, the thinking and behaviors of churches and church leaders must adjust to these new realities. Communication and mapping are more dynamic than ever before. To thrive in this environment, leaders must become experts in improvising. If they are to remain effective, pastors must become proficient as team leaders, learning to welcome, enjoy, and even prefer change over the status quo.[2]

The first skills that must be improved and adjusted are in communication. In our consultations, one of the most frequent complaints is about communication within the church. People object to outdated and ineffective forms of communication. On the other hand, new communication systems have created another problem—too much communication and too much information availability. We are in input overload, being bombarded with input from multiple sources—television, radio, Internet, and other media.

But a more serious communication problem is insufficient two-way communication of vision—what is going on in the church and why. When people don't understand what the leadership team is doing, serious consequences often result. The problem is that change is hard to navigate and adopt when church members sense that their needs and concerns are not being considered seriously.

In one affluent, mainline congregation, this perception had risen to a dangerous point, with many people resisting an aggressive strategy for shifting resources into urban ministries. Several key families withdrew their financial support. The primary problem in that instance was not the quality or integrity of the strategic mapping process but that too little attention had been given to communication. Consequently, the congregation was having a hard time understanding the motives and actions of its leaders. After working for several months, though, on improving the communication process and listening to and valuing people's input, the strategy was resumed with widespread support.

When an acceptable level of two-way communication was reached, people were happier and more committed. Many of that church's perceived "problems" disappeared once effective communication took place. The people in the congregation could concentrate on developing and carrying out their mission rather than getting bogged down in "vain imaginings."

Another reason for poor communication is the way information is transmitted. As a message flows down a communication channel, meaning can be dissipated or lost. At the top level, information is shared with 100 percent of the leaders. In turn, the information is communicated down to the next level of leaders, but they hear only 90 percent of the original message. Then they tell the people below them, but they understand only about 67 percent of the original communication. The process continues until the congregation hears only about 30 percent (see fig. 12.1).

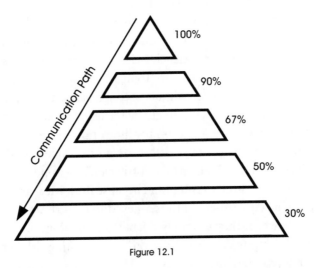

Figure 12.1

Most of us have experienced such communication failure by playing a simple game. First, one person whispers a message in the ear of another person. That person then passes the message along to a third person, who in turn passes it along quietly to another. The process continues until the last person in the chain hears the message, then tells the group what he or she heard. It is often, as we all know, a very different message than was spoken in the ear of the first person.

For some reason, the farther a message is passed along, the greater the misunderstanding. Thus, church leaders must do their best to communicate directly to all members, even those on the fringe. A lot of trouble can result when people on the edge hear something and say, "Not in my church."

The key, of course, is repetition. Consider what happens when you first hear a commercial for a fast food restaurant. In most cases, you immediately forget the commercial. Yet, after you've heard the commercial several times, you begin singing the jingle! Effective communication within the church in a time of complexity requires multiple types, styles, and pathways to get the message through *and* understood. A message cannot be repeated often enough.

The second skill that relates to change is being able to determine the church's *core issues.* In the new millennium, leadership teams must quickly identify those issues that have the greatest impact upon their constituencies, either favorably or adversely. *A core issue is an issue that matters.* It might be related to an internal obstacle, something from within the congregation that is preventing forward progress. Or it might be related to an external factor over which the leadership team has little or no control.

Sometimes the core issues that are most difficult to identify are "opportunities" rather than "obstacles." An opportunity often arises with little warning, and because the leaders are so preoccupied with other matters, they don't sense its strategic importance, or they're simply unable to respond in time.

Leadership teams that thrive on change distinguish between secondary issues and core issues. They address the core issues quickly. They do not get bogged down in uncertainty or disagreements concerning how best to resolve the issue. They first conduct an analysis of the situation, then articulate a series of clear, realistic action steps. Once they address an issue, the leadership team moves on to other matters.

The extent to which a congregation is healthy, growing, and reproductive depends largely upon how well leadership teams are able to identify and address core issues. Some issues can be overwhelming for teams that lack experience, prefer to avoid facing issues, or deny their existence. When leadership teams are able to enjoy identifying and addressing issues, they have shifted from resisting to thriving on change.

There's never a time when an individual or a congregation no longer has core issues. The only question is whether that person or congregation knows which issues are core issues and whether they have the courage and means to address them. Addressing core issues and gathering momentum go hand in hand. Leadership teams that thrive on change are like the little train that struggled with its first few "chug, chugs," but then eventually reached an optimum pace. The Holy Spirit has placed within each leadership team sufficient collective wisdom to address any core issue. We all have blind spots, and no one has 20/20 vision in complex situations, except the teamlike Godhead of the Father, Son, and Holy Spirit.

A third skill that is essential for this new turbulent environment is span of care, or limiting the number of persons under the direct care of a leader. As discussed earlier, most pastors are spinning too many plates and falter seriously because they believe they need to care for all of their leaders personally and directly. Jethro was the first trusted advisor to identify this phenomenon. He told Moses, "The thing that you are doing is not good. You will surely wear out" (Exod. 18:17–18). All pastors need to hear Jethro's wisdom and solution. Jethro gave Moses a crisp set of solutions: "Select . . . able men who fear God, men of truth, those who hate dishonest gain; and you shall place these over them as leaders of thousands, of hundreds, of fifties and of tens" (v. 21).

In the most advanced leadership teams today, we see this same pattern. In fractal teams, for example, the span of care for each team facilitator is four people, plus the spouse or friend of each of those members. Altogether, that makes ten (one plus four, times two, equals ten).

It's no coincidence that with these optimal spans of care, the quality of the relationships and the level of productivity are both outstanding. Almost all of the resourcing and authority flow through these intimate relationships of trust. Communication is greatly increased, and only rarely do issues arise that need to be resolved outside of each team. Not only is this biblically mandated span of care superior to the corporate models of command and control but also it has once again made those models officially obsolete.

Questions to Consider

1. What might be the result if your church were able to cut at least in half its reaction time to new problems and began to see them as opportunities that are caused by external changes?
2. How can you develop a communication system that allows people to feel part of what the church is about and be able to contribute their giftedness?
3. What kind of positive impact would this have on the ability of the congregation to fulfill its mission?
4. How much difference would this impact have on morale and the momentum of your ministry?

Case Study 10

Thriving on Change:
Mosaic Southern Baptist
Los Angeles, California

Only one church appears twice in these case studies, and it is Mosaic. They are the undisputed leader in a number of life-giving systems. No other church so naturally morphs than Mosaic. They don't have to work at breaking out of an institutional box as most congregations do. Creativity oozes from every pore.

Both up close and over a period of several years, I (Dan) have witnessed them repeatedly take change in stride. It's in their nature. They resist falling into routine and refinement, unless it will increase their global impact in obeying Christ's mandate to a lost and broken world. They prefer the raw and spontaneous over the refined. Certainly, most postmoderns resonate with this new beat.

The leaders at Mosaic now understand the responsibility they have to nurture the movement that is being drawn to Erwin McManus's prophetic writings. They have committed to make their annual leadership conference, "Origins," in May, a high priority. One of the most impressive aspects of Mosaic's ministry is their approach to change—they raise the standard for leadership roles higher rather than lower it. Many other leaders tend to settle for the lowest common denominator. Erwin and Alex McManus, along with the rest of their discerning team, understand that as churches grow, the new people coming into the circle are farther and farther away from the apostolic ethos at the core. To compensate for this distance, Mosaic keeps raising rather than lowering the cost of discipleship, making it more dangerous (realistic and compelling) and less comfortable.

Conclusion

Liftoff

Our Lord's promise in Matthew, "I will build My church" (16:18), is as immediate today as it was two thousand years ago. If Christ does not return during the next few years, this passage will continue to be a primary source of comfort and directive for twenty-first-century congregations.

The church of the twenty-first century, however, will not be the same church that Christ commissioned during His post-Resurrection appearances. Both the terrain and the audience have vastly changed. The mission of Christ's church, however, continues constant: to make and send disciples. But the church cannot ignore a second, implicit task of revitalizing congregations that are stuck in neutral or stagnated in unhealthful circumstances.

The Great Commission obligates us to assign top priority to church growth through planting new congregations. The condition of the average church, though, as well as the redeeming work of Christ, requires us to work toward redevelopment of existing congregations. Church leaders recognize that the challenge of redevelopment is so intense that it often saps the energy that could (and should) be invested in church planting.

Our culture conditions us, however, to cut corners in an effort to find the secret for growing a healthy church. In the era of one-minute managers, church leaders are constantly looking for *the* answer to reviving a church. The growth and health of churches, however, is a complex matter. Despite the proliferation of health-indicator tools, no single answer for developing a healthy church exists.

Nevertheless, a common denominator can be observed in every growing church. It is the interaction between all of the life-giving systems about which this book discusses. When each life-giving system becomes healthy and effective, it often has a ripple effect on the rest of the life-giving systems. On its own, however, each life-giving system is incomplete. In the physical body, the parts are designed to interact and work together to produce a healthy whole. So in the church, intercession interacts with mobilization, organizational streamlining affects people flow, and so on. When enough of the life-giving systems become healthy, the synergy is unstoppable—a church experiences new health and vitality; the negative forces holding it back are driven out of the system.

As might be suspected, although the common denominator in a growing church is easy to identify, the results are not nearly as easy to produce. One of the primary challenges facing congregations that desire to be faithful concerns the matching of resources to the church's needs. Growing congregations excel at finding resources and matching them to their unique needs. The odds are quite low, however, that any single congregation will discover the right combinations of resources on its own. However, two factors, more than any others, seem to increase the odds.

First, struggling and ineffective churches may find help by looking at the "best practices" of thriving churches.[1] Visit some churches and observe how they treat you as a visitor. Interview other churches' members and find out what they like about their church. Identify how the life-giving systems function in that church. Do not, however, try merely to import or copy models from other churches. You may pick up some good ideas by visiting and interviewing, but God wants you to have a unique identity, not a copied identity. Trying to import and duplicate models, especially from well-known churches, will be disappointing because church models are not "plug and play." A church's life and strategies should arise from an analysis of and a response to the situation of each. Every church, like each individual, has a unique identity. Therefore, each church needs a unique strategy, one that is developed out of its own DNA, to pull together all of its life-giving systems.

Second, more will be required of the average church than merely desiring to grow and looking at best practices. Increasing evidence from both pastors and denominational executives shows that finding a ministry coach can help a church fulfill its mission. In many instances, growth will not happen unless someone with coaching skills comes alongside the congregation's leaders. Ministry coaches bring the knowledge and perspective that enable churches to build teams to accomplish the desired growth and health.

A great deal is at stake in revitalizing the life-giving systems of a church. Leaders who dedicate themselves to improving ministry operations will find great personal fulfillment. Watching a ministry "liftoff" produces an emotional and spiritual high that even exceeds winning a sports championship. Nothing can match the joy of watching people finding Christ in the context of a healthy, harmonious, and vision-inspired church. A church with healthful life-giving systems provides a ground for growing new disciples and unleashes them to advance rapidly in their faith and become leaders.[2]

The majority of congregations in the United States must choose during the next several years between a slow, agonizing death or a fruitful, abundant harvest. No viable alternative and very little middle ground remains. Leaders who have determined to be part of the harvest are already positioning their churches for revitalizing each life-giving system. They are on the alert for fresh ministry opportunities that will enable them to lift off. On the other hand, leaders who hesitate too long likely will miss the greatest opportunity in several generations to influence their world.

Most congregations face serious and profound issues that need to be overcome if they are to share in the coming harvest. And that harvest can, indeed, be a big one. If you as a church leader are ready to become part of it, join us (Gary and me) in building churches with healthful life-giving systems.

Let's shout from rooftops the warning to get ready for the Big One! But let us be equally diligent in praying for and working together toward as many congregations as possible experiencing liftoff—whereby Christ can be lifted up with power and grace.

Questions to Consider

1. Which life-giving system is the healthiest in your church?
2. Which one seems to need the most help?
3. What are you going to do in the next few weeks to begin building healthful life-giving systems in your church?
4. How might you benefit from having a ministry coach to meet with each month?

Endnotes

Introduction: There's a Whole Lot of Shaking Going On

1. Peter F. Drucker, *Post-Capitalist Society* (New York: Harper, 1993), 1.
2. Tom Peters, *The Tom Peters Seminar: Crazy Times Call for Crazy Organizations* (New York: Vintage, 1994), 8.
3. Joel Barker, *Discovering the Future: The Business of Paradigms* (St. Paul, MN: ILI Press, 1989), 2–3.
4. Lyle Schaller, *Strategies for Change* (Nashville: Abingdon, 1993), 10–11.
5. Leith Anderson, *A Church for the Twenty-first Century: Bringing Change to Your Church to Meet the Challenges of a Changing Society* (Minneapolis: Bethany House, 1992), 17.
6. For an excellent introduction to Wesley's innovative approaches, see Howard A. Snyder, *The Radical Wesley* (Eugene, OR: Wipf and Stock, 1996).
7. Quoted by Hector Tobar and Miles Corwin, "Blackout Shows the Reach of Technology into Daily Life," *Los Angeles Times,* 12 August 1996, A26.
8. Ibid.
9. Quoted by Eric Slater and Ricardo Alonso-Zaldivar, "The Nation: Millions of Paths to Blackout," *Los Angeles Times,* 19 August 2003, A8.

10. The blackened cover of the September 19, 2005 edition of *Time* magazine simply stated "System Failure," as it gave one of the early assessments of what went wrong in responses to Hurricane Katrina, the nation's most spectacular functional breakdown, three weeks earlier. The feature article reported four areas where the system broke down and hobbled the government at all levels. Less than a week later, an equally dangerous Hurricane Rita struck east Texas near the Louisiana border reinforcing the vulnerability of the most basic systems of water, electricity, police protection, traffic flow, housing, and jobs.

11. Many of my (Dan) experiences in American churches were discouraging in the years immediately following my return from Europe. Hope returned during the 80s at the Fuller Institute with the opportunity to blend missiological theories from my doctoral studies with emerging theories from the social sciences in high impact congregational settings. Important clues came from studying classic texts such as H. G. Barnett, *Innovation: The Basis of Cultural Change* (New York: McGraw-Hill, 1953); Donald McGavran, *The Bridges of God* (New York: Friendship Press, 1955); James MacGregor Burns, *Leadership* (New York: HarperCollins, 1978); Charles Kraft, *Christianity in Culture* (New York: Orbis, 1979); Edwin Friedman, *Generation to Generation: Family Process in Church and Synagogue* (New York: Guildford Press, 1985); and Anne Wilson Schaef and Diane Fassel, *The Addictive Organization* (San Francisco: Harper and Row, 1988). Systemic concepts were then adapted, tested, and refined during leadership retreats with high potential, motivated congregations.

12. These life-systems concepts were further refined during the 90s when the field of systems thinking was popularized for church practitioners by a diverse field of researchers. The primary contributors were Bernard Bass, *Leadership and Performance Beyond Expectations* (New York: Free Press, 1985); Chris Argyris, *Overcoming Organizational Defenses* (Boston: Harvard University, 1990); Peter M. Senge, *The Fifth Discipline: The Art and Practice of the Learning Organization* (New York: Doubleday, 1990); Daniel Kim, *Systems Archetypes I, II and Systems Thinking Tools* (Cam-

bridge, MA: Pegasus Communication, 1992–95); George Parson and Speed Leas, *Understanding Your Congregation as a System* (Bethesda, MD: Alban Institute, 1993); Phillip Lewis, *Transformational Leadership: A New Model for Total Church Involvement* (Nashville: Broadman and Holman, 1994); Norman Shawchuck and Roger Heuser, *Managing the Congregation: Building Effective Systems to Serve People* (Nashville: Abingdon, 1996); and Peter Steinke, *Healthy Congregations: A Systems Approach* (Bethesda, MD: Alban Institute, 1996).

13. For other relevant systemic approaches to congregational revitalization, see Jim Herrington, Mike Bonem, and James Furr, *Leading Congregational Change: A Practical Guide for the Transformational Journey* (San Francisco: Jossey-Bass, 2000) and Alan McMahan, "Training Turn-Around Leaders: Systemic Approaches to Reinstating Growth in Plateaued Churches" (Ph.D. diss., School of World Mission, Fuller Theological Seminary, 1998). An insightful unpublished work containing systems theory, which McMahan also refers to, is Hans Finzel, "A Descriptive Model for Discerning Organizational Culture" (Ph.D. diss., School of World Mission, Fuller Theological Seminary, 1989).

14. In a book with more than 200 pages of ideas, the thesis can easily be missed. Yet the threads for this systems revolution, with "the interaction of the parts" at its heart, run deep into the past century. As far as we know the original thinking is attributed to Ludwig von Bertalanffy. During the mid 1920s this practicing biologist was able to challenge the prevailing Newtonian method in science, which assumed that the whole of a system could be understood by examining each of the parts without considering the relationship of the parts. As Bertalanffy began to understand living organisms in a systems way and to view them as a complex whole, he was able to articulate the counter principle that neither the whole nor the parts can be understood unless the interrelationships of the parts are understood (from Paul Stevens and Phil Collins, *The Equipping Pastor: A Systems Approach to Congregational Leadership* [Bethesda, MD: Alban Institute, 1993], xxi. For the original material, see Ludwig von Bertalanffy, *Perspectives on*

General Systems Theory: Scientific-Philosophical Studies [New York: George Braziller, 1968], 12.)

Chapter 1: Societal Quakes Affecting the Twenty-First-Century Church

1. When I (Dan) completed my doctorate in missiology twenty-five years ago, it was rare to find a pastor in America who knew what the word "cross-cultural" meant, or who could comprehend why cross-cultural communication of the gospel was relevant to growing a healthy church. Today the awareness has greatly increased. Some of the best places to start are Eugene Nida, *Message and Mission: The Communication of the Christian Faith* (Pasadena, CA: William Carey, 1960); Roland Allen, *Missionary Methods, St. Paul's or Ours?* (Grand Rapids: Eerdmans, 1962); Louis Luzbetak, *The Church and Cultures* (Techny, IL: Divine Word Publications, 1970); Tetsunao Yammamori and Charles Taber, *Christopaganism or Indigenous Christianity* (Pasadena, CA: William Carey, 1975); Dean S. Gilliland, *Pauline Theology and Mission Practice* (Eugene, OR: Wipf and Stock, 1998); Paul Hiebert, *Missiological Implications of Epistemological Shifts: Affirming Truth in a Modern/Postmodern World* (Harrisburg, PA: Trinity, 1999); and George Hunter, *The Celtic Way of Evangelism, How Christianity Can Reach the West . . . Again* (Nashville: Abingdon, 2000).

2. Books on societal shifts since 1990 are too numerous to list. Here is a sampling: Glen Martin and Gary McIntosh, *The Issachar Factor* (Nashville: Broadman and Holman, 1993); Leonard Sweet, *FaithQuakes* (Nashville: Abingdon, 1994); Donald Miller, *Reinventing American Protestantism: Christianity in the New Millennium* (Los Angeles: University of California, 1997); Michael Riddell, *Threshold of the Future: Reforming the Church in the Post-Christian West* (London: SPCK, 1998); Lyle Schaller, *Discontinuity and Hope: Radical Change and the Path to the Future* (Nashville: Abingdon, 1999); Steve Rabey, *In Search of Authentic Faith: How Emerging Generations Are Transforming The Church* (Colorado Springs: WaterBrook Press, 2001); George Barna, *The Second Coming of the Church* (Nashville: Word, 1998); Chuck Smith, Jr., *The*

End of the World as We Know It: Clear Direction for Bold and Innovative Ministry in a Postmodern World (Colorado Springs: WaterBrook Press, 2001); Thomas Bandy, *Fragile Hope: Your Church in 2020* (Nashville: Abingdon, 2002); Reggie McNeal, *The Present Future: Six Tough Question for the Church* (San Francisco: Jossey-Bass, 2003); Michael Frost and Alan Hirsch, *The Shaping of Things to Come: Innovation and Mission for the 21st Century Church* (Peabody, MA: Hendrickson, 2003); Peter Wagner, *Changing Church: How God Is Leading His Church Into the Future* (Ventura, CA: Regal, 2004); Rex Miller, *The Millennium Matrix: Reclaiming the Past, Reframing the Future of the Church* (San Francisco: Jossey-Bass, 2004); and Jim Wilson, *Future Church: Ministry in a Post-Seeker Age* (Nashville: Broadman and Holman, 2004).

3. "These Christians Radically Rethink What a Church Is," *Los Angeles Times,* 14 August 2004.

Chapter 2: Toxic Terrain, Hot Air Balloons, and Spinning Plates

1. There are lots of other "ropes and weights" that could potentially keep churches grounded. Gary and I (Dan) have more than a hundred possible factors we consider in most consultations. Often some of the weightier and more stubborn items that need removing in congregations are not readily apparent on the surface. Most consultants use Lyle Schaller, *The Interventionist* (Nashville: Abingdon, 1997) as their introductory manual.

2. Some leadership teams are looking for proven strategies that are easy to understand. Although no strategies will work in every situation, three of the clearest and most universal approaches that I have seen outlined for getting to liftoff on a sure and steady path are: Thom Rainer, *Eating the Elephant: Bite-Sized Steps To Achieve Long-Term Growth In Your Church* (Nashville: Broadman and Holman, 1999); Rick Warren's, *The Purpose Driven Church: Growth Without Compromising Your Message and Mission* (Grand Rapids: Zondervan, 1995); and Andy Stanley, Reggie Joiner, and Lane Jones, *Seven Practices of Effective Ministry* (Sisters, OR: Multnomah, 2004). Other approaches will be introduced in later chapters.

3. Church members often have predetermined expectations of

pastors, as far as how they should spend their time, or which of their many roles are the most important. During the last decade pastors have become more aware of their giftedness. Most of them would probably consider this factor to be more important than others' expectations of how they should allocate their time. Since the unprecedented reaction to Rick Warren's best-selling book, *The Purpose Driven Life: What on Earth Am I Here For?* (Grand Rapids: Zondervan, 2002), leaders are more keenly aware of the need to be focused and to operate primarily in the areas that match their divine shape. Tom Paterson's LifePlanning process relates closely to *The Purpose Driven Life*. Tom Paterson was a helpful mentor to Rick Warren in the decade that preceded this book. A description of this LifePlanning process can be found in *Living the Life You Were Meant to Live*, (Nashville: Thomas Nelson, 1998).

Chapter 3: Life-Giving System 1: Pastor's Spiritual Life

1. For one such study, see C. Peter Wagner, *Leading Your Church to Growth* (Ventura, CA: Regal, 1984).
2. Kent Hunter, "The Church with Ten Windows," *Journal of the American Society for Church Growth* 13 (Fall 2002): 15.
3. See also Bill Easum, *Put On Your Own Oxygen Mask First: Rediscovering Ministry* (Nashville: Abingdon, 2004), and Robert Quinn, *Deep Change: Discovering the Leader Within* (San Francisco: Jossey-Bass, 1996).
4. Thomas G. Bandy, *Road Runner: The Body in Motion* (Nashville: Abingdon, 2002), 33–37.
5. Alan Nelson, *Embracing Brokenness: How God Refines Us Through Life's Disappointments* (Colorado Springs: NavPress, 2002). This text was published originally under the title *Broken in the Right Place*.

Chapter 4: Life-Giving System 2: Corporate Intercession

1. Some helpful resources can be found in C. Peter Wagner, *Prayer Shield* (Ventura, CA: Regal,1992); C. Peter Wagner, *Churches that Pray* (Ventura, CA: Regal, 1993); Randall Roth, *Prayer Powerpoints* (Wheaton, IL: Victor, 1995); and Bill Bright, *Joy of Active Prayer* (Wheaton, IL: Victor, 2005).

Chapter 5: Life-Giving System 3: Spiritual Disciplines

1. See Dallas Willard, *The Divine Conspiracy: Rediscovering Our Hidden Life in God* (San Franciso: HarperCollins, 1998); Dallas Willard, *Renovation of the Heart: Putting on the Character of Christ* (Colorado Springs: NavPress, 2002); Eugene Peterson, *A Long Obedience in the Same Direction: Discipleship in an Instant Society* (Downers Grove, IL: InterVarsity, 2000); Richard Foster, *Celebration of Discipline: The Path to Spiritual Growth* (San Francisco: Harper & Row, 1978); and Douglas Rumford, *SoulShaping: Taking Care of Your Spiritual Life* (Wheaton, IL: Tyndale House, 1996).

2. Kevin Mannoia, *The Integrity Factor: A Journey in Leadership Formation* (Indianapolis: Light and Life, 1996), 30–32.

Chapter 6: Life-Giving System 4: Mentoring Relationships

1. Paul D. Stanley and J. Robert Clinton, *Connecting: The Mentoring Relationships You Need to Succeed in Life* (Colorado Springs: NavPress, 1992), 162.

2. Jack Dennison, *City Reaching* (Pasadena, CA: W. Carey Library, 1999).

3. Tom Paterson, *Living the Life You Were Meant to Live* (Nashville: Nelson, 1998). For an updated version of Tom's process, called LifeMapping, visit IMLT.org.

4. Rick Warren, *The Purpose Driven Life: What on Earth Am I Here For?* (Grand Rapids: Zondervan, 2002).

5. Another classic booklet on mentoring, the first to impact my (Dan) European mentoring of leaders, is Douglas Hyde, *Dedication and Leadership Techniques* (Washington, DC: Mission Secretariat, 1966). See also, Bob Buford, *Game Plan: Winning Strategies for the Second Half of Your Life* (Grand Rapids: Zondervan, 1998).

Chapter 7: Life-Giving System 5: Team Ministry

1. Ralph Winter and R. Pierce Beaver, *The Warp and the Woof* (Pasadena, CA: William Carey, 1970).

2. Kenneth Scott Latourette, *A History of Christianity*, vol. 1, *Beginnings to 1500,* rev. ed. (1953; repr., San Francisco: HarperCollins, 1975), 333.

3. For a compelling argument to support this thesis, see Greg Ogden, *The New Reformation* (Grand Rapids: Zondervan, 1990).

4. Stephen L. Schey and Walt Kallestad, *Team Ministry: A Workbook for Getting Things Done* (Nashville: Abingdon, 1996), 111. For the best examples of missional teams in congregational settings, see Erwin R. McManus, *An Unstoppable Force: Daring to Become the Church God Had in Mind* (Loveland, CO: Group, 2001); and Wayne Cordeiro, *Doing Church as a Team* (Ventura, CA: Regal Books, 2001). For more evidence of the theology of teams in Scripture, see George Cladis, *Leading the Team-Based Church: How Pastors and Church Staffs Can Grow Together into a Powerful Fellowship of Leaders* (San Francisco: Jossey-Bass, 1999). Two introductory texts on team ministry are E. Stanley Ott, *Transform Your Church with Ministry Teams* (Grand Rapids: Eerdmans, 2004), and Roger Heuser, ed., *Leadership and Team Building: Transforming Congregational Ministry Through Teams* (Matthews, NC: Christian Ministry Resources, 1999).

Having stated my (Dan) concerns about building teams in churches based upon corporate models rather than New Testament missional models, here are a few supplementary texts for advanced practitioners: Patrick Lencioni, *The Five Dysfunctions of a Team: A Leadership Fable* (San Francisco: Jossey-Bass, 2002); Jean Lipman-Blumen and Harold J. Leavitt, *Hot Groups: Seeding Them, Feeding Them and Using Them to Ignite Your Organization* (Oxford: Oxford University Press, 1999); Dorothy Leonard and Walter Swap, *When Sparks Fly: Igniting Creativity in Groups* (Boston: Harvard Business School Press, 1999); Warren Bennis and Patricia Ward Biederman, *Organizing Genius: The Secrets of Creative Collaboration* (Reading, MA: Addison-Wesley, 1997); and Harvey Robbins and Michael Finley, *Why Teams Don't Work: What Went Wrong and How to Make It Right?* (Princeton, NJ: Peterson's/Pacesetter Books, 1995).

Chapter 8: Life-Giving System 6: People-Flow Strategy

1. R. Daniel Reeves and Ronald Jenson, *Always Advancing: Modern Strategies for Church Growth* (San Bernardino, CA: Here's Life, 1984), 67–89.

2. This people-flow strategy builds upon the missiological models of James Engel, Alan Tippett, Donald McGavran, Peter Wagner, John Wimber, and Ralph Winter. Wimber's process of finding, folding, feeding, forming, and fielding is worth highlighting. The model was developed during the mid-1970s and is still relevant one generation later. Simple questions can be asked for each of the "f-verbs." For example, where does this function occur in our current people-flow strategy? For a detailed description of these various models, see Reeves and Jenson, *Always Advancing.*

3. For organizations, articles, and other current church planting approaches, see Church Planting Resources Table at www .mislinks.or/church/chplant.htm. For a radical, streamlined approach to church planting, see Neil Cole, *The Organic Church: Growing Faith Where Life Happens* (San Francisco: Jossey-Bass, 2005).

4. For a clear front-door sequence see Stanley, Joiner, and Jones, *Seven Practices of Effective Ministry.*

5. For side-door approaches see Steve Sjogren, *Conspiracy of Kindness* (Ann Arbor, MI: Servant Publications, 1993); George G. Hunter III, *How to Reach Secular People* (Nashville: Abingdon, 1992); George G. Hunter III, *Radical Outreach* (Nashville: Abingdon, 2003); Lewis Drummond, *Reaching Generation Next: Effective Evangelism in Today's Culture* (Grand Rapids: Baker, 2002); and Rick Rusaw and Eric Swanson, *The Externally Focused Church* (Loveland, CO: Group, 2004). For missiological support of an external shift in focus, see Johannes Blauw, *The Missionary Nature of the Church* (New York: McGraw-Hill, 1962); Richard DeRidder, *Discipling the Nations* (Grand Rapids: Baker, 1975); John Bright, *The Kingdom of God* (Nashville: Abingdon, 1953); Charles Van Engen, *God's Missionary People: Rethinking the Purpose of the Local Church* (Grand Rapids: Baker, 1995); Howard Snyder, ed., *Global Good News: Mission in a New Context* (Nashville: Abingdon, 2002); and Arthur F. Glasser, *Announcing the Kingdom: the Story of God's Mission in the Bible* (Grand Rapids: Baker, 2003).

Chapter 9: Life-Giving System 7: Lifestyle Evangelism

1. For ideas on how to serve your community, see Steve Sjogren, *101 Ways to Reach Your Community* (Colorado Springs: NavPress, 2001).

2. See Win and Charles Arn, *The Master Plan for Making Disciples* (Grand Rapids: Baker, 1982, 1998). See also, Bill Hybels and Mark Mittelberg, *Becoming a Contagious Christian* (Grand Rapids: Zondervan, 1995).

3. For a proven approach to lifestyle evangelism, see Bill Bright, *The Joy of Sharing Jesus: You Have A Story to Tell* (Wheaton, IL: Victor, 2005).

Chapter 10: Life-Giving System 8: Charting the Future

1. Henry Mintzberg's study in the mid-1990s initiated a sea change of skepticism for professional planners (*The Rise and Fall of Strategic Planning: Reconceiving Roles for Planning, Plans, and Planners*, [New York: Free Press, 1994]).

2. A good introduction to dynamic and interactive mapping is Bill Easum, *Leadership On the Other Side: No Rules, Just Clues* (Nashville: Abingdon, 2000). See also Thomas Bandy, *Moving Off the Map: A Field Guide to Changing the Congregation* (Nashville: Abingdon, 1998) and Bill Easum, *UnFreezing Moves: Following Jesus into the Mission Field* (Nashville: Abingdon, 2001).

3. There is in fact considerable confusion over the nature, function, and mission of the church. Numerous books in the fields of ecclesiology and missiology have attempted to bring clarity since 1990. Most of the breakthroughs are occurring at the local level within individual congregations. The most important strategic question for leadership teams is "With whom in the Body of Christ do we primarily identify?" Here is a selection of authors to help you sort through the various issues: Donald Bloesch, *The Church: Sacraments, Worship, Ministry, Mission* (Downers Grove, IL: InterVarsity, 2002); Veli-Matti Kärkkäinen, *An Introduction to Ecclesiology: Ecumenical, Historical and Global Perspectives* (Downers Grove, IL: InterVarsity, 2002); Johannes A. van der Ven, *Ecclesiology in Context* (Grand Rapids: Eerdmans, 1993); Howard

Snyder, *Decoding the Church: Mapping the DNA of Christ's Body* (Grand Rapids: Baker, 2002); Erwin McManus, *An Unstoppable Force: Daring to Become the Church God Had in Mind* (Loveland, CO: Group Publishing, 2001); Ed Delph, *Church@Community: Strategic Core Values that Engage Faith in Culture* (Lake Mary, FL: Creation House Press, 2005); Mike Breen and Walt Kallestad, *The Passionate Church: The Art of Life-Changing Discipleship* (Colorado Springs: Cook Communications, 2005); and Neil Cole, *Organic Church, Growing Faith Where Life Happens* (San Francisco: Jossey-Bass, 2005).

4. This warning to avoid copying is no longer just good advice; it is essential to long-term survival. Wayne Cordeiro puts it this way, "Hammer your own trumpet!" For both the rationale and the process for discerning your own identity see, Robert Lewis and Wayne Cordeiro, *Culture Shift: Transforming Your Church From the Inside Out* (San Francisco: Jossey-Bass, 2005), 37–124.

Chapter 11: Life-Giving System 9: Streamlining the Organization

1. I (Dan) am indebted to my friend and colleague, Daniel Allen, for help in researching and drafting parts of this chapter from a wide range of literature.

2. For an overview, see Gary McIntosh, *Staff Your Church for Growth: Building Team Ministry in the 21st Century* (Grand Rapids: Baker, 2000).

3. For additional description of the fractaling approach, see "Building Teams," in Wayne Cordeiro, *Doing Church as a Team*, (Ventura, CA: Regal, 2004), 172–190.

Chapter 12: Life-Giving System 10: Thriving on Change

1. Two books by Eddie Gibbs will assist in understanding and addressing this increasingly complex field of ministry known as the local church: *ChurchNext: Quantum Changes in How We Do Ministry* (Downers Grove, IL: InterVarsity, 2000) and *Leadership Next: Changing Leaders in a Changing Culture* (Downers Grove, IL: InterVarsity, 2005).

2. Tom Peters sounded the original alarm in the corporate world with

his 1987 best-seller, *Thriving on Chaos: Handbook for Management Revolution* (San Francisco: HarperCollins, 1987). Leith Anderson echoed the call from church rooftops in 1990 with *Dying for Change* (Minneapolis: Bethany House). Then there was an avalanche of books and articles that followed, including: William Bridges, *Managing Transitions: Making the Most of Change* (Reading, MA: Addison-Wesley, 1991); Lyle Schaller, *Strategies for Change* (Nashville: Abingdon, 1993); John Kotter, *Leading Change* (Boston: Harvard Business School Press, 1996); Lyle Schaller, *The Interventionist* (Nashville: Abingdon, 1997); James White, *Rethinking the Church: A Challenge to Creative Redesign in an Age of Transition* (Grand Rapids: Baker, 1997); and Thomas Bandy, *Coaching Change: Breaking Down Resistance, Building Up Hope* (Nashville: Abingdon, 2000). By the turn of the millennium the need for change had been embraced by most churches. Resources became bolder and more focused. See, for example, John Jackson, *Pastorpreneur: Pastors and Entrepreneurs Answer the Call,* (Friendswood, TX: Baxter Press, 2003); Robert Quinn, *Building the Bridge as You Walk on It: A Guide for Leading Change* (San Francisco: Jossey-Bass, 2004); George Barna, *Revolution* (Wheaton, IL: Tyndale, 2005); and Erwin McManus, *The Barbarian Way: Unleash the Untamed Faith Within* (Nashville: Thomas Nelson, 2005).

Chapter 13: Liftoff

1. For a tour of the most promising innovative churches see: Bill Easum and Dave Travis, *Beyond the Box: Innovative Churches That Work* (Loveland, CO: Group, 2003); Rick Rusaw and Eric Swanson, *The Externally Focused Church* (Loveland, CO: Group, 2004); Bill Easum and Pete Theodore, *The Nomadic Church: Growing Your Congregation Without Owning the Building* (Nashville: Abingdon, 2005); and Bill Easum and Bill Tenny-Brittian, *Under The Radar: Learning From Risk-Taking Churches* (Nashville: Abingdon, 2005).

2. We can assist in helping you find the right coach. Between the two of us we do most types of congregational coaching. We are also networked with dozens of other specialist coaches across the country.

Resources

Bandy, Thomas. *Road Runner: The Body in Motion.* Nashville: Abingdon, 2002.

Breen, Mike, and Walt Kallestad. *The Passionate Church: The Art of Life-Changing Discipleship.* Colorado Springs, CO: Cook Communications, 2005.

Cole, Neil. *Organic Church: Growing Faith Where Life Happens.* San Francisco: Jossey-Bass, 2005.

Cordeiro, Wayne. *Doing Church as a Team: The Miracle of Teamwork and How It Transforms Churches.* Ventura, CA: Regal, 2004.

Easum, Bill. *Put on Your Own Oxygen Mask First: Rediscovering Ministry.* Nashville: Abingdon, 2004.

Easum, Bill, and Bil Cornelius. *Go BIG: Leading Your Church to Explosive Growth.* Nashville: Abingdon, 2006.

Easum, Bill, and Dave Travis. *Beyond the Box: Innovative Churches That Work.* Loveland, CO: Group, 2003.

Frost, Michael, and Alan Hirsch. *The Shaping of Things to Come: Innovation and Mission for the 21st-Century Church.* Peabody, MA: Hendrickson Publishers, 2003.

Gibbs, Eddie. *ChurchNext: Quantum Changes in How We Do Ministry.* Downers Grove, IL: InterVarsity, 2000.

———. *LeadershipNext: Changing Leaders in a Changing Culture.* Downers Grove, IL: InterVarsity, 2005.

Gibbs, Eddie, and Ryan Bolger. *Emerging Churches: Creating Christian Community in Postmodern Cultures*. Grand Rapids: Baker Academic, 2005.

Haggard, Ted. *The Life-Giving Church*. Ventura, CA: Regal, 1997.

Hunter, George G., III. *The Celtic Way of Evangelism: How Christianity Can Reach the West . . . Again*. Nashville: Abingdon, 2000.

———. *Church for the Unchurched*. Nashville: Abingdon, 1996.

———. *How to Reach Secular People*. Nashville: Abingdon, 1992.

———. *Radical Outreach: The Recovery of Apostolic Ministry and Evangelism*. Nashville: Abingdon, 2003.

Hunter, Kent R. *Move Your Church to Action*. Nashville: Abingdon, 2000.

Kinnaman, Gary D., and Alfred H. Ells. *Leaders That Last: How Covenant Friendships Can Help Pastors Thrive*. Grand Rapids: Baker, 2003.

Lewis, Robert. *The Church of Irresistible Influence*. Grand Rapids: Zondervan, 2001.

Lewis, Robert, and Wayne Cordeiro. *Culture Shift: Transforming Your Church From the Inside Out*. San Francisco: Jossey-Bass, 2005.

McGavran, Donald. *The Bridges of God*. Pasadena, CA: Fuller Seminary Press, 1997.

McIntosh, Gary L. *Biblical Church Growth*. Grand Rapids: Baker, 2003.

———. *The Exodus Principle*. Nashville: Broadman and Holman, 1995.

———. *One Size Doesn't Fit All*. Grand Rapids: Baker, 1999.

McIntosh, Gary L., and Glen S. Martin. *Finding Them, Keeping Them*. Nashville: Broadman, 1992.

McManus, Erwin Raphael. *The Barbarian Way: Unleash The Untamed Faith Within*. Nashville: Thomas Nelson, 2005.

———. *An Unstoppable Force: Daring to Become the Church God Had in Mind*. Loveland, CO: Group, 2001.

———. *Uprising: A Revolution of the Soul*. Nashville: Nelson, 2003.

Miller, Rex. *The Millennium Matrix: Reclaiming the Past, Reframing the Future of the Church*. San Francisco: Jossey-Bass, 2004.

Quinn, Robert. *Building the Bridge as You Walk on It: A Guide for Leading Change*. San Francisco: Jossey Bass, 2004.

Rainer, Thom. *The Unchurched Next Door*. Grand Rapids: Zondervan, 2003.

Reeves, R. Daniel, and Ronald Jenson. *Always Advancing: Modern Strategies for Church Growth*. San Bernardino, CA: Here's Life, 1984.

Scazzero, Peter. *The Emotionally Healthy Church*. Grand Rapids: Zondervan, 2003.

Schaller, Lyle E. *Activating the Passive Church*. Nashville: Abingdon, 1981.

———. *Discontinuity and Hope: Radical Change and the Path to the Future*. Nashville: Abingdon, 1999.

———. *The Interventionist*. Nashville: Abingdon, 1997.

Shogren, Steve. *Changing the World Through Kindness*. Ventura, CA: Regal, 2005.

Snyder, Howard. *Decoding the Church: Mapping the DNA of Christ's Body*. Grand Rapids: Baker, 2002.

Stark, Rodney. *The Rise of Christianity: How the Obscure, Marginal Jesus Movement Became the Dominant Religious Force in the Western World in a Few Centuries*. San Francisco: HarperCollins, 1997.

Sweet, Leonard. *Aqua Church*. Loveland, CO: Group, 1999.

Towns, Elmer, and Ed Stetzer. *Perimeter of Light: Biblical Boundaries for the Emerging Church*. Chicago: Moody, 2004.

Van Engen, Charles. *God's Missionary People*. Grand Rapids: Baker, 1991.

Wagner, C. Peter. *Changing Church*. Ventura, CA: Regal, 2004.

Werning, Waldo. *God Says, "Move!"* Lima, OH: Fairway, 1997.

Winter, Ralph, and R. Pierce Beaver. *The Warp and the Woof*. Pasadena, CA: William Carey, 1970.

Services Available

DR. GARY L. MCINTOSH speaks to numerous churches, organizations, schools, and conventions each year. Services available include keynote presentations at major meetings, as well as conducting seminars and workshops, training courses, and ongoing consultation and coaching.

For a live presentation of the material found in this book or to request a catalog of materials or other information on Dr. McIntosh's availability and ministry contact him at garymcintosh@kregel.com

DR. R. DANIEL REEVES provides consultation, training, mentoring, and coaching for individuals, local congregations, pastor and leadership-team networks, denominations, and movements. Dan is available for consultation regarding the critical points and systems introduced in this book, as well as consultation in new services regarding the development of leadership teams and shifting to teams at congregational and denominational levels.

Dr. Reeves also offers a LifeMapping service for individuals who want to fully use and focus their gifts and talents in all areas of their lives and ministries, and he provides a LifeSystems approach for strategic mapping that helps groups, churches, and denominations who want to prepare themselves fully for twenty-first-century ministry.

Contact Dan at danreeves@kregel.com

About the Authors

Dr. Gary L. McIntosh is a nationally known author, speaker, educator, consultant, and Professor of Christian Ministry and Leadership at Talbot School of Theology, Biola University, in La Mirada, California. He has written extensively in the field of pastoral ministry, leadership, generational studies, and church growth.

Dr. McIntosh received his B.A. degree in Biblical Studies from Colorado Christian University, an M.Div. degree from Western Seminary in Pastoral Studies, a D.Min. degree in Church Growth Studies from Fuller Theological Seminary, and a Ph.D. in Intercultural Studies from Fuller Theological Seminary.

As president of The Church Growth Network, a church consulting firm he founded in 1989, Dr. McIntosh has served more than 750 churches in fifty-five denominations throughout the United States and Canada. The 1995 and 1996 President of the American Society for Church Growth, he edits both the *Growth Points* newsletter and the *Journal of the American Society for Church Growth.*

Dr. McIntosh is a veteran pastor, having served for fifteen years as a youth pastor, Christian education director, and senior pastor. During the early 1980s, he was vice president of consulting services for the influential Institute for American Church Growth in Pasadena, California. For the past twenty years, Dr. McIntosh has been a professor of Christian Ministry and Leadership at Talbot School of Theology, Biola University, in La Mirada, California.

Dr. R. Daniel Reeves is a missiologist, consultant, and director of the Institute of Missional Leadership Teams. For more than twenty-five years he has led cross-cultural missional teams, and has coached and mentored pastors, congregations, and consultants. Dan has had practical experience in the United States and Europe as a mission and denominational executive, pastor, professor, and business owner, and is a published author whose books and articles are often used for graduate courses and training leadership teams.

Dr. Reeves received his B.A. degree in social science and business from Westmont College, in Santa Barbara, California. He and his wife later led pioneer ministry teams among students and churches for seven years in Europe, living in London and France. He earned his master's and doctoral degrees in missiology from Fuller Seminary's School of World Mission in Pasadena and spent ten years working cross-denominationally with the Fuller Institute in Pasadena, California, which was then widely recognized as the premier consulting resource for American congregations. Later, he began working independently, refining the LifeSystems approach to strategic mapping, and, in addition performed consultations to single churches, pioneering and refining various network "clusters" for pastors and leadership teams in small and midsized churches. His primary consulting emphasis now is coaching churches in transition, LifeMapping, and team ministry.

In the mid-1990s, Dan served as president of the American Society of Church Growth. In 1997, he founded the Council on Ecclesiology, which developed out of a deep concern over the unnecessary fragmentation among various streams of Christianity. Dr. Reeves has been the convener and facilitator for the council since its inception, bringing together such diverse groups as Willow

Creek, Mosaic, *Christianity Today*, New Apostolic Reformation, and the Alliance of Confessing Evangelicals as well as young leaders and inner-city pastors to work through the core issues concerning the nature, function, and mission of the church.

Subject Index